Kindle

Paperwhite

User Guide

A Complete Manual with Tips and Tricks for Beginners and Seniors to Master Your Kindle E-Reader

Alexander Thorne

Table of Contents

Introduction to the Kindle Paperwhite 5

Why Choose the Kindle Paperwhite? 7

Chapter 1 9

Getting Started 9

Unboxing and Initial Setup ⁚.............................. 9

Overview of Specifications 11

Chapter 2 15

Basic Hardware and Features 15

Exploring the Kindle Paperwhite's Design 15

Understanding Status Indicators 18

Chapter 3 21

Setting Up Your Kindle Paperwhite 21

Step-by-Step Device Setup 21

Network Connectivity 24

Managing Saved Wi-Fi Passwords 27

Chapter 4 33

Navigating Your Kindle Paperwhite 33

Using the Home Screen 33

Voice-View Screen Reader for Accessibility. 37

Navigating a Book 43

Using Kindle Page Flip 48

Navigating with the "Go To" Button 53

Chapter 5 59

Enhancing Your Reading Experience 59

Adjusting Font, Brightness, and Themes 59

Using Vocabulary Builder and Word Wise 64

Highlighting, Notes, and Bookmarks 68

Chapter 6 75

Advanced Features 75

How to Add Multiple Accounts 75

Understanding Device and Cloud Storage 80

Managing Your Kindle Content 87

Chapter 7 95

Content Management 95

Downloading and Deleting Books 95

Organizing Your Library with Collections 101

Transferring Content from an Old Kindle to Your New One
.... 107

Chapter 8 115

Maintenance and Care 115

Cleaning and Maintaining Your Kindle Paperwhite 115

Tips to Minimize Interference 122

Chapter 9 129

Safety and Compliance 129

    Important Safety Tips for Using Your Device................ 129

    Regulatory Information.. 136

Chapter 10... 143

Troubleshooting and Support.................................... 143

    Common Issues and Solutions...................................... 143

    Resetting Your Kindle Paperwhite 150

    Contacting Amazon Support.. 154

Frequently Asked Questions (FAQ) 161

Introduction to the Kindle Paperwhite

Have you ever wondered how to make the most of your Kindle Paperwhite? Perhaps you've asked questions like:

- How do I set up my Kindle Paperwhite for the first time?
- What's the best way to navigate through a book or manage my library?
- Can I transfer my old Kindle books to a new device?
- What should I do when my Kindle encounters connectivity issues?
- Are there hidden features that can elevate my reading experience?

If these questions resonate with you, you're not alone. As an experienced Kindle Paperwhite user, I've encountered these questions countless times, both as a curious beginner and a seasoned reader. The Kindle Paperwhite is more than just an e-reader; it's a powerful, feature-rich device designed to bring your literary adventures to life. However, unlocking its full potential requires a bit of guidance—especially for those who are new to the Kindle ecosystem or transitioning from another e-reader.

This user guide is your trusted companion to navigating everything the Kindle Paperwhite has to offer. From basic setup and hardware tips to advanced features like navigating with Page Flip or using VoiceView for accessibility, this book covers it all. You'll learn how to organize your library, manage multiple accounts, and even troubleshoot common issues like a pro.

Whether you're a casual reader looking to enjoy your favorite novels or a serious bookworm eager to explore advanced tools, this guide is crafted to make your Kindle Paperwhite journey seamless and enjoyable. With clear instructions, step-by-step guides, and helpful tips drawn from real-world experience, you'll gain the confidence to use your Kindle like an expert.

So, let's dive in. By the end of this book, you'll not only have answers to your questions but also a deeper appreciation for the remarkable technology in your hands. Your Kindle Paperwhite adventure begins here!

Why Choose the Kindle Paperwhite?

The Kindle Paperwhite stands out as one of the most popular and versatile e-readers on the market, blending cutting-edge technology with a user-friendly design. But what makes it the go-to choice for readers worldwide?

First and foremost, the Kindle Paperwhite offers an unparalleled reading experience. Its high-resolution display with 300 PPI mimics the look of real paper, ensuring crisp, clear text without the glare of traditional screens—even in bright sunlight. Whether you're reading under a sunny sky or in a dimly lit room, the adjustable front light ensures perfect readability, day or night.

Another key advantage is its portability. With a sleek, lightweight design and weeks-long battery life, the Paperwhite is perfect for avid readers on the move. It allows you to carry thousands of books in your pocket, eliminating the need for bulky paperbacks or heavy hardcovers.

The Kindle Paperwhite also caters to modern reading needs, offering waterproof protection for poolside or bathtub reading, robust storage options, and seamless integration with Kindle's vast library of eBooks. Whether you prefer classic novels or the latest bestsellers, the Paperwhite ensures instant access to your favorite titles.

For readers who value convenience, comfort, and an immersive experience, the Kindle Paperwhite is a clear winner. It's not just an e-reader—it's a gateway to limitless literary exploration.

Chapter 1

Getting Started

Unboxing and Initial Setup

Unboxing your Kindle Paperwhite is an exciting first step into a world of endless reading possibilities. Amazon has designed the packaging to be sleek and minimal, ensuring a smooth and straightforward unboxing experience.

As you open the box, you'll find the Kindle Paperwhite itself carefully nestled within. The device's slim, lightweight design immediately stands out, showcasing the craftsmanship that has gone into creating a premium e-reader. Alongside the Kindle, you'll find a USB charging cable and a quick-start guide to help you get started. While a power adapter isn't included, the USB cable can be plugged into any standard adapter or USB port for charging.

Before powering up your device, take a moment to remove the protective film covering the screen. Once ready, press and hold the power button located at the bottom edge of the Kindle. After a few seconds, the Paperwhite logo will appear, signaling that your device is booting up.

The initial setup process is straightforward and user-friendly. Upon turning on the device, you'll be prompted to select your preferred language. Next, connect your Kindle to a Wi-Fi network by following the on-screen instructions. This step is essential for downloading books, syncing your library, and accessing Kindle features.

You'll also be asked to log in to your Amazon account or create a new one if you're a first-time user. Logging in links your device to your Kindle library, giving you immediate access to any previously purchased eBooks.

Finally, you'll have the option to customize your device settings, such as font size, screen brightness, and theme preferences. Once setup is complete, you're ready to explore your Kindle Paperwhite's features and start building your digital library.

Unboxing and setting up your Kindle Paperwhite is more than just a task—it's the beginning of a transformative reading journey.

Overview of Specifications

The Kindle Paperwhite is renowned for its thoughtful design and advanced features, making it a favorite among e-reader enthusiasts. Below is an overview of the key specifications that set this device apart:

Display

- **Screen Type**: 6.8-inch glare-free display
- **Resolution**: 300 PPI (pixels per inch) for crisp, laser-quality text
- **Lighting**: Adjustable front light with 17 LED lights and a warm light option for a comfortable reading experience day or night
- **Technology**: E-Ink Carta technology for a paper-like reading experience, even in direct sunlight.

Design and Build

- **Dimensions**: Compact and lightweight, ideal for one-handed reading
- **Waterproofing**: IPX8 rating, designed to withstand accidental splashes or immersion in water, perfect for poolside or bathtub reading

- **Materials**: Durable, sleek design with a smooth, ergonomic finish

Performance

- Storage: Options of 8GB or 32GB, capable of storing thousands of books, audiobooks, or PDFs
- Battery Life: Lasts up to 10 weeks on a single charge, depending on usage
- Processor: Optimized for seamless page-turning and smooth navigation

Connectivity

- **Wi-Fi**: Supports both 2.4GHz and 5GHz networks for fast, reliable downloads
- **Optional Cellular**: Some models offer free 4G LTE for book downloads on the go

Additional Features

- **Accessibility**: VoiceView screen reader support for visually impaired users
- **Content Compatibility**: Supports eBooks, PDFs, and audiobooks (via Bluetooth)
- **Integration**: Syncs effortlessly with your Amazon account and Kindle ecosystem

Eco-Friendly Design

Sustainability: Made with 60% post-consumer recycled plastics

This well-rounded blend of technology and user-centric design makes the Kindle Paperwhite a must-have device for readers seeking convenience, comfort, and innovation in their e-reading experience.

Chapter 2

Basic Hardware and Features

Exploring the Kindle Paperwhite's Design

The Kindle Paperwhite's design is a perfect blend of elegance, functionality, and durability. Every aspect of its construction is crafted to enhance the reader's experience, making it a top choice for book lovers who value convenience and style.

Slim and Lightweight Build

The Kindle Paperwhite is impressively slim and lightweight, designed to be portable and easy to hold for hours without causing strain. Its compact size makes it ideal for slipping into a bag or even a jacket pocket, ensuring you can carry your library wherever you go.

Matte Finish for Comfort

The device features a matte, soft-touch finish that not only feels premium but also provides a comfortable grip, even during long reading sessions. The smooth edges and minimalist design add to its ergonomic appeal.

6.8-Inch E-Ink Display

At the heart of the Kindle Paperwhite's design is its stunning 6.8-inch E-Ink display. The screen is flush with the bezel, creating a sleek, modern look while making navigation seamless. With 300 PPI resolution, text appears crisp and clear, closely resembling the quality of printed paper. The glare-free screen ensures readability even under direct sunlight.

Adjustable Lighting

The device is equipped with 17 LED lights, offering even illumination across the screen. The addition of a warm light setting allows you to switch between white and amber tones, reducing eye strain during nighttime reading.

Waterproof Construction

The Kindle Paperwhite is built to withstand real-life scenarios, including accidental splashes or full submersion in water. Its IPX8 waterproof rating ensures you can confidently use it near pools, at the beach, or in the bathtub.

USB-C Port for Charging

The inclusion of a USB-C port simplifies charging, allowing for faster, more efficient power-ups.

Minimalistic Aesthetic

The Kindle Paperwhite features a single power button and an otherwise clean, button-free exterior, emphasizing its sleek, clutter-free design.

Eco-Friendly Materials

Amazon has taken a sustainable approach, crafting the Kindle Paperwhite with 60% post-consumer recycled plastics, making it an environmentally conscious choice.

The Kindle Paperwhite's thoughtful design not only elevates the reading experience but also demonstrates the perfect balance between aesthetics and functionality. It's a device you'll be proud to own and eager to use.

Understanding Status Indicators

The Kindle Paperwhite's status indicators play a crucial role in helping users understand the device's current state and functioning. These subtle yet essential signals keep you informed about the device's power, connectivity, and overall performance, ensuring a seamless reading experience.

Power Indicator Light

Located near the power button, the power indicator light provides important information about your device's battery and charging status:

- **Solid Green**: The battery is fully charged.
- **Solid Amber**: The device is currently charging.
- **No Light**: The Kindle is in use and has sufficient battery, or it's powered off.
- **Blinking Amber or Green**: Indicates a potential issue with charging or the device.

Wi-Fi and Network Connectivity

The status bar on the Kindle Paperwhite's screen is where you can find connectivity indicators:

- **Wi-Fi Symbol**: Displays the strength of the Wi-Fi connection. More bars indicate stronger connectivity, which is important for downloading books or syncing your library.
- **Airplane Mode Icon**: Appears when the device is offline, saving battery by disconnecting from all networks.
- **4G/LTE Indicator (on cellular models)**: Shows when cellular connectivity is active for downloading books on the go.

Battery Status

The battery icon in the upper-right corner of the screen provides real-time updates on battery life:

- **Full Icon**: Indicates a fully charged battery.
- **Depleting Icon**: The battery is being used; recharge is needed soon.
- **Low Battery Warning**: Alerts you when the battery is critically low, prompting immediate charging.

Reading Progress Indicators

While reading, you'll notice additional indicators at the bottom of the screen:

- **Time Left in Chapter/Book**: An estimate based on your reading speed.
- **Page Location or Percentage Completed**: Helps you track where you are in the book.

Software Updates and Notifications

When your Kindle requires an update or has a notification, an alert may appear in the status bar or home screen. Keeping the software updated ensures optimal performance.

By understanding these status indicators, you can stay informed about your Kindle Paperwhite's functionality and troubleshoot minor issues effectively. This knowledge ensures you're always prepared to enjoy your reading experience without interruptions.

Chapter 3

Setting Up Your Kindle Paperwhite

Step-by-Step Device Setup

Setting up your Kindle Paperwhite for the first time is an exciting process that will quickly have you reading your favorite books. The setup is intuitive, and within a few simple steps, you'll be ready to explore the vast Kindle library. Here's a detailed guide to help you through the initial setup:

Step 1: Power On the Device

To begin, press and hold the power button, located on the bottom edge of the Kindle Paperwhite. After a few seconds, the Amazon logo will appear, signaling that the device is turning on. Once powered up, you'll be greeted by the welcome screen.

Step 2: Select Your Language

The first screen will ask you to choose your preferred language. Simply select your language from the list, and tap "Next" to proceed.

Step 3: Connect to Wi-Fi

To start using your Kindle, you'll need an active Wi-Fi connection. On the Wi-Fi setup screen, choose your network from the available list and enter your Wi-Fi password. If you're unsure about the password, double-check your router or ask your network administrator for the details. A strong connection ensures faster downloads and smoother syncing.

Step 4: Sign In to Amazon Account

Once connected to Wi-Fi, the next screen will prompt you to log in to your Amazon account. If you already have one, enter your credentials (email and password). If you don't have an Amazon account, you can create one during the setup process. This step is essential, as logging in links your Kindle Paperwhite to your existing library and gives you access to Amazon's vast catalog of eBooks, audiobooks, and magazines.

Step 5: Sync Your Library

After logging in, your Kindle will sync with your Amazon account, automatically downloading any books or content you've previously purchased. This process may take a few minutes, depending on the size of your library and the strength of your Wi-Fi connection.

Step 6: Customize Your Kindle Settings

Once your device is set up and synced, you can begin customizing it to suit your reading preferences. You can adjust font size, screen brightness, and text alignment. You can also choose the reading theme (dark or light mode) or enable features like Kindle's accessibility tools, such as VoiceView for visually impaired users.

Step 7: Start Reading

Now that your Kindle Paperwhite is all set up, it's time to start reading! You can browse the Kindle Store, explore free sample chapters, or download books you've already purchased. The user-friendly interface allows you to search for books by title, author, or genre, making it easy to build your digital library.

By following these simple steps, you've now set up your Kindle Paperwhite and are ready to enjoy a seamless and immersive reading experience. The device is designed to ensure that you can start reading almost immediately, without a complicated setup process. Enjoy your new Kindle Paperwhite, and happy reading!

Network Connectivity

The Kindle Paperwhite offers seamless network connectivity to ensure you can access your library, purchase new books, and sync your reading progress from anywhere. Whether you're at home, in a café, or traveling, understanding how to connect and manage your device's network settings is crucial to maintaining a smooth and uninterrupted reading experience. Here's everything you need to know about the Kindle Paperwhite's network connectivity:

Connecting to Wi-Fi

Wi-Fi is the primary method for connecting your Kindle Paperwhite to the internet, and it's essential for downloading books, syncing content, and browsing the Kindle Store.

1. Initial Connection: During the initial setup, the Kindle Paperwhite will prompt you to connect to a Wi-Fi network. Simply select your network from the available list, enter your password, and tap "Connect." This ensures that your device is ready to access online content and services.

2. **Managing Wi-Fi Networks**: To manage Wi-Fi settings, swipe down from the top of the screen to access the Quick Actions menu, then tap the Wi-Fi icon. From here, you can connect to a new network, disconnect from the current network, or forget a network you no longer use. If you're in an area with weak Wi-Fi, try moving closer to the router for a stronger signal.

3. **Wi-Fi Strength Indicator**: At the top of the screen, a Wi-Fi icon will appear to show the strength of the connection. The more bars displayed, the better the connection. A strong Wi-Fi signal is crucial for quick downloads and smooth syncing with your Amazon account.

Connecting via 4G (Cellular Model)

If you own the Kindle Paperwhite with 4G LTE capability, you can connect to Amazon's network without needing Wi-Fi. This feature is especially useful for downloading books or syncing content while on the go.

Automatic Connection

The 4G model will automatically connect to the 4G LTE network when you're not near a Wi-Fi network. There's no need for a separate mobile plan or data charges since Amazon provides free 4G access for downloading Kindle books.

Cellular Icon

When connected via 4G LTE, the cellular signal icon will appear in the status bar at the top of the screen. You can check the strength of the cellular connection in the same way you would check the Wi-Fi signal.

Airplane Mode

When you need to disconnect from all wireless networks to save battery or avoid interruptions, you can use Airplane Mode. To activate it, swipe down from the top of the screen and tap the Airplane Mode icon. In this mode, your Kindle will not connect to Wi-Fi or cellular networks, but you can still read offline content.

Troubleshooting Connectivity Issues

Occasionally, you might experience connectivity issues, such as trouble connecting to Wi-Fi or slow download speeds. Here are some common solutions:

- **Restart Your Kindle**: A simple restart can often resolve minor connection issues.
- **Forget and Reconnect to Wi-Fi**: Go to your Wi-Fi settings, forget the current network, and reconnect by entering the password again.
- **Check Router Settings**: Ensure your router is functioning properly and there are no network outages.
- **Reset Network Settings**: If all else fails, reset your Kindle's network settings and start the connection process from scratch.

With these easy-to-follow steps, managing network connectivity on your Kindle Paperwhite will be a breeze. Whether you're using Wi-Fi or 4G LTE, you'll always have quick access to the Kindle Store, updates, and your content library, ensuring a smooth and enjoyable reading experience.

Managing Saved Wi-Fi Passwords

The Kindle Paperwhite simplifies your reading experience by allowing you to seamlessly connect to Wi-Fi networks, but what happens when you need to manage saved Wi-Fi passwords? Whether you're moving to a new location, reconnecting to a network, or troubleshooting connectivity issues, understanding how to manage and update your saved Wi-Fi passwords ensures smooth access to your Kindle account and online features. Here's how you can manage your saved Wi-Fi passwords on your Kindle Paperwhite:

Viewing Saved Wi-Fi Networks

Your Kindle Paperwhite remembers the Wi-Fi networks you've connected to in the past, allowing you to reconnect automatically when you're in range. To view and manage saved Wi-Fi networks:

1. **Access Wi-Fi Settings**: Swipe down from the top of the screen to open the Quick Actions menu, then tap on the Wi-Fi icon. This will open the list of available networks. If your device is connected to a network, the active connection will appear at the top.

2. **Manage Saved Networks**: At the bottom of the list of available Wi-Fi networks, tap on **"Saved Networks"** or **"Wi-Fi Settings"**. Here, you'll see a list of all previously connected networks.

Forgetting a Network

If you no longer want your Kindle Paperwhite to automatically connect to a particular network, you can choose to forget the network. This is useful when you switch to a different Wi-Fi provider or no longer need to connect to a certain network. To forget a network:

1. In the **Saved Networks** section, find the Wi-Fi network you wish to remove.

2. Tap on the network name, then select **"Forget"** from the options.

3. Confirm your choice. Once forgotten, your Kindle will no longer connect to that network unless you manually re-enter the password.

Updating a Saved Wi-Fi Password

If the password for a network changes (e.g., after a router reset or password update), you'll need to update it on your Kindle Paperwhite to reconnect. Unfortunately, the Kindle Paperwhite does not allow you to edit the password directly from the saved networks list. Instead, you'll need to remove the old network and reconnect with the new password:

1. Forget the Old Network: Go to the **Saved Networks** list, select the network, and choose **"Forget"** as described earlier.

2. Reconnect with the New Password: After forgetting the old network, return to the Wi-Fi settings and select the network again. Enter the new password when prompted, and your Kindle will save the new credentials for future use.

Managing Multiple Networks

If you regularly move between different locations, such as work, home, and public spaces, your Kindle Paperwhite will remember up to a few networks at a time. You can easily switch between them in the Wi-Fi settings. Simply select the desired network from the list, enter the password if required, and your Kindle will connect.

Troubleshooting Wi-Fi Connectivity

If you encounter issues with your saved Wi-Fi network, try the following:

- **Reboot Your Kindle**: A restart can resolve connection issues and refresh saved settings.
- **Re-enter Password**: If the saved password is not working, manually enter the password again after selecting the network.
- **Check Router Settings**: Ensure your router is working properly and that there are no signal interferences or outages.

- **Forget and Reconnect**: If there's persistent trouble with a saved network, forgetting it and reconnecting fresh can often resolve problems.

Chapter 4

Navigating Your Kindle Paperwhite

Using the Home Screen

The Kindle Paperwhite's home screen is your central hub for navigating through your library, discovering new books, and managing settings. Understanding how to effectively use the home screen will help you quickly access your content and make the most of your device. Here's a detailed guide on how to use and customize the Kindle Paperwhite home screen:

Overview of the Home Screen Layout

Upon powering on your Kindle Paperwhite, the home screen will display the following key elements:

1. Top Navigation Bar:

- **Search Icon**: Located in the upper-left corner, this allows you to quickly search for books, authors, or genres.
- **Menu Icon**: On the upper-right, the three vertical dots represent the menu, where you can access settings, sync your device, manage content, and perform other tasks.
- **Wi-Fi Status**: The Wi-Fi icon indicates whether you're connected to a network.
- **Battery Icon**: The battery status is displayed here, showing the remaining charge and battery life.

2. Bookshelf: The main area of the home screen displays your **Bookshelf**—a visually organized list of books and content currently stored on your Kindle. Each title is represented by a cover image and the title of the book. The most recently opened books are shown first. You can scroll horizontally to see more titles, especially if you have a large library.

3. Reading Progress Bar: Beneath each book's cover image, you'll find a progress bar showing how far you are in your current read. This helps you quickly pick up where you left off without needing to open the book.

4. Collections If you've organized your books into collections, you can view these as separate sections or groups on the home screen. This feature allows you to categorize books by genre, reading status (e.g., "To Read" or "Currently Reading"), or other personalized groupings.

5. Recommendations and Store: At the bottom of the home screen, you'll find **Recommended for You** and **Explore** sections. These offer personalized book suggestions based on your reading history. Below that, the Kindle Store button allows you to browse and shop for new books, magazines, and audiobooks.

Navigating the Home Screen

Using the Kindle Paperwhite's home screen is as simple as tapping and swiping:

- **Tap on a Book to Open**: To open a book, tap its cover on the Bookshelf. You'll instantly be taken to the last page you read.
- **Swipe Left/Right to Browse**: Swipe left or right across the screen to move between books and explore new content. This is especially useful if you have a lot of books in your library.
- **Long Press for Options**: Long-press on a book title for additional options, like removing it from

the device, managing collections, or sharing the book via Goodreads or social media.

Customizing Your Home Screen

You can personalize the Kindle Paperwhite's home screen to suit your needs:

1. Sort Your Library: In the top menu, you can choose how to sort your books. Options include sorting by title, author, or most recent. You can also opt to display books in a grid or list view.

2. Creating Collections: Tap on the menu icon in the top-right corner of the home screen, and select **"Create a New Collection"** to organize books into categories. You can assign books to multiple collections, making it easy to find what you're looking for.

3. Turn Off Recommendations: If you prefer not to see the recommended titles on the home screen, you can disable this feature from the **Settings** menu under **Device Options > Advanced Options**.

4. Syncing Your Content: From the menu icon, select **Sync My Kindle** to ensure that your content, notes, and progress are updated across all devices connected to your Amazon account.

Other Key Features

- **Accessing Archived Books**: If you've removed a book from your Kindle Paperwhite, you can access it via the **Cloud** section on the home screen. Tap on the **Cloud** icon to view and download books that are stored in your Amazon account but not currently on your device.
- **Switching Between Devices**: If you use multiple devices to read (like a phone or tablet), your Kindle Paperwhite will sync with your Amazon account to ensure that you can continue reading from where you left off.

The home screen of the Kindle Paperwhite is designed to provide easy access to all of your content while allowing for a personalized experience. With a few taps and swipes, you can organize your library, discover new books, and enjoy seamless reading across multiple devices.

Voice-View Screen Reader for Accessibility.

The Kindle Paperwhite includes a powerful feature called **VoiceView**, a screen reader designed to enhance accessibility for users with visual impairments. By reading aloud the text on your Kindle's screen, VoiceView allows you to navigate, read books, and use the Kindle Paperwhite with ease, ensuring that all users can enjoy the immersive reading experience. Here's a detailed guide on how to activate and use the VoiceView screen reader.

What is VoiceView?

VoiceView is a built-in text-to-speech feature that reads aloud the content displayed on the Kindle Paperwhite screen. It reads not only the text of your books but also the menus, settings, and other on-screen elements, making it easier for those with visual impairments to interact with the device. VoiceView uses the device's built-in speakers or any connected Bluetooth audio device, such as headphones or a speaker, to play the audio.

Activating VoiceView

To activate VoiceView, follow these steps:

1. Turn on Your Kindle Paperwhite: Press and hold the power button to turn on your Kindle.

2. Access Accessibility Settings: Swipe down from the top of the screen to open the Quick Actions menu. Tap on **"Settings"**.

3. Enable VoiceView:

In the **Settings** menu, select **"Accessibility"**.

From the Accessibility menu, tap **"VoiceView Screen Reader"** and switch the toggle to "On".

Your Kindle Paperwhite will prompt you to confirm that you want to enable VoiceView. Tap **"Enable"**.

Once VoiceView is activated, it will start reading the text on the screen aloud. If you're in a book, it will begin reading from the current page or location.

Using VoiceView

After VoiceView is enabled, you can interact with your Kindle Paperwhite using touch gestures and auditory feedback:

1. Navigating the Kindle Screen:

- **Swipe Right**: Move to the next item on the screen.
- **Swipe Left**: Move to the previous item on the screen.

- **Double Tap**: Select an item (e.g., open a book, activate a button).
- **Swipe Up/Down**: These gestures allow you to adjust settings like reading speed and volume.

2. Reading a Book:

- Once a book is open, VoiceView will read the text aloud. You can pause and resume the reading by tapping the screen.
- **Swipe Right** to go to the next paragraph or page, and **Swipe Left** to go back.
- **VoiceView** reads aloud both the text and any navigational elements, such as the page numbers, chapter titles, and the progress bar.

3. Adjusting the Reading Speed:

- Swipe down from the top of the screen and tap **"Settings"**.
- Select **"Accessibility"**, then tap **"VoiceView Settings"**.
- Here, you can adjust the **reading speed** and **voice selection**. You can choose between different available voices and alter the speed to suit your preference.

4. Navigating Menus: VoiceView will also read aloud the options and settings in menus. For example, if you're in the Kindle Store, it will read the titles and buttons, helping you navigate to the book you wish to purchase or download.

5. Turning Off VoiceView: To disable VoiceView, go back to **Settings > Accessibility > VoiceView Screen Reader** and toggle it off. You can also press and hold the power button to turn off the screen reader if you need a break from audio feedback.

VoiceView with Bluetooth Devices

For a more immersive experience, you can connect your Kindle Paperwhite to Bluetooth headphones or a speaker. This is particularly useful in noisy environments or when you want private listening. To connect a Bluetooth device:

1. Go to Settings: Swipe down from the top and select **"Settings"**.

2. Pair Bluetooth Device: Tap **"Bluetooth"**, and ensure that Bluetooth is turned on. Then, pair your Kindle with your Bluetooth headphones or speaker from the list of available devices.

Once connected, VoiceView will play through your Bluetooth device, offering clearer audio for an enhanced reading experience.

Benefits of VoiceView

VoiceView makes Kindle Paperwhite an accessible device for users who are blind or have low vision. Some key benefits include:

- **Independent Reading**: Users can read their eBooks aloud without needing additional assistance.
- **Navigating Content**: The ability to navigate the Kindle interface and content makes it easy to explore, browse, and read books.
- **Accessibility Everywhere**: Whether at home, on a bus, or in a park, users can enjoy reading via VoiceView, which works seamlessly with both Wi-Fi and cellular models of Kindle Paperwhite.

VoiceView opens up a world of possibilities for users with visual impairments, making the Kindle Paperwhite an inclusive and versatile device. By enabling the screen reader, adjusting settings, and learning the gestures, you can enjoy a fully immersive reading experience. Whether you're navigating your library, reading a book, or exploring new titles, VoiceView provides an invaluable tool for accessibility and enjoyment.

Navigating a Book

Navigating through a book on the Kindle Paperwhite is designed to be intuitive and user-friendly, making it easy for you to move through pages, chapters, and sections without losing your place. Whether you're looking for a specific part of the text, want to jump to a new chapter, or are reading for a while and want to take a break, the Kindle Paperwhite offers several convenient features to enhance your reading experience. Here's how to navigate a book on the Kindle Paperwhite:

Basic Page Navigation

Once you've opened a book, you'll find the following methods of navigation:

1. **Swipe or Tap to Turn Pages**: The most common method of navigating a book is to **swipe** left or right to move between pages. Alternatively, you can **tap** near the right side of the screen to go forward a page, or on the left side to go back to the previous page. This is the primary way to move through the content when you're simply reading from start to finish.

2. **Using the Progress Bar**: At the bottom of the screen, you'll see a progress bar showing your current position in the book. Tap on the progress bar to bring up a detailed view of the current chapter and a slider that allows you to quickly jump to a specific location in the book. This is particularly helpful if you want to skip ahead or go back to a specific point without having to swipe through every page.

3. **Page Numbers and Location**: Kindle Paperwhite offers two ways to track your progress: **Page Numbers** (if the book includes them) or **Location**. The page numbers are traditional references, while location numbers are unique to Kindle's format. Both are displayed at the top or bottom of the screen, depending on your settings. If you prefer one over the other, you can switch between them in the **Reading Settings**.

Navigating Chapters and Sections

To easily move between different parts of the book:

1. **Go To Button**: The **Go To** button provides an efficient way to navigate directly to specific chapters, sections, or locations in the book. Tap the top of the screen to bring up the menu, then select **Go To**. You'll be presented with several options:

- **Table of Contents**: Quickly jump to the start of any chapter.
- **Location**: Type a specific location or chapter number to go directly there.
- **Bookmarks**: If you've bookmarked certain parts of the book, you can jump directly to those spots.
- **Search**: Search within the book for a specific word, phrase, or chapter.

2. **Using the Table of Contents**: For books with a **Table of Contents**, you can access it from the **Go To** menu. This is especially helpful for reference books or multi-chapter novels, as you can quickly navigate to a specific chapter, section, or part of the book. Simply tap on a chapter title to be taken directly to that section of the book.

Bookmarks and Highlights

The Kindle Paperwhite allows you to mark important passages, making it easy to return to them later:

1. **Bookmarking Pages**: To bookmark a page, tap the top of the screen to open the menu, then select **Bookmark**. A small icon will appear on the page to indicate that it's been marked. You can access all your bookmarks by going to the **Go To** menu and selecting **Bookmarks**.

2. **Highlighting Text**: If you come across a passage you want to remember or annotate, you can highlight text by tapping and holding on a word, then dragging to select the desired passage. Afterward, a menu will appear offering options to highlight, add a note, or share the passage. You can view all your highlights by accessing the **Your Notes and Highlights** section in the **Go To menu**.

Using Kindle Page Flip

Kindle Page Flip is a useful feature for browsing through a book while keeping your place. This feature allows you to flip through pages without losing your spot:

1. **Activate Page Flip**: Tap on the top of the screen to bring up the menu, and select **Page Flip**. Once activated, you can swipe through pages without the risk of losing your current location in the book. A mini preview of each page will appear on the screen, making it easier to skim through the text. When you find the section you're looking for, tap on the page to return to your previous location.

2. **Pinpointing a Specific Page**: When you're in **Page Flip**, you can also use the **Go To** feature to directly navigate to any page, chapter, or location in the book.

Reading Tools for Ease of Navigation

The Kindle Paperwhite includes additional tools that make navigating your book even more convenient:

1. **Text Size and Layout**: If you find it difficult to read, you can adjust the text size, font, and line spacing by tapping on the top of the screen to access the **Aa** (font) menu. This allows you to customize the reading experience to suit your preferences.

2. **Night Mode**: For those who prefer reading in low light, you can activate **Night Mode** by adjusting the brightness or selecting the dark background in the **Reading Settings**. This helps reduce eye strain and enhances visibility in dim environments.

3. **X-Ray Feature**: The **X-Ray** feature is available for many books and provides a way to dive deeper into the characters, terms, and concepts mentioned throughout the book. You can access X-Ray from the **Go To** menu to view detailed information about specific topics.

Navigating with Kindle Page Flip and the Go To Button

Page Flip and the **Go To** button are powerful tools that let you explore a book without interrupting your reading flow. While Page Flip provides an intuitive way to move through pages and sections visually, the **Go To** button provides direct access to chapters, locations, and specific bookmarks for more precise navigation. Together, they help you engage with your book in the most efficient and personalized way.

Using Kindle Page Flip

Kindle Page Flip is a powerful and convenient feature designed to help you navigate through your eBooks without losing your place. Whether you're skimming through a book for a specific section, comparing two parts of the text, or just browsing, Page Flip makes the process smooth and intuitive. Here's how to use the Kindle Paperwhite's Page Flip feature effectively:

What is Kindle Page Flip?

Page Flip is a feature that allows you to "flip" through the pages of a book while keeping your current reading position intact. It provides a mini-preview of the pages you're navigating through, so you can easily jump between sections without losing your spot. This is particularly useful when you're looking for a specific piece of information or revisiting a previously read passage without flipping back and forth repeatedly.

Activating Kindle Page Flip

To start using Page Flip, follow these simple steps:

1. Open a Book: Begin by opening any eBook on your Kindle Paperwhite.

2. Enable Page Flip:

- Tap on the **top of the screen** to bring up the toolbar.
- Select the **Page Flip icon** (represented by a small, circular arrow or a page icon). This activates the Page Flip feature, allowing you to freely browse through the book's pages while keeping your current position.

  Once activated, you'll see a mini preview of the pages you're flipping through at the bottom of the screen. These thumbnails allow you to quickly scan through content and find the specific section you're looking for.

Navigating with Page Flip

Once Page Flip is enabled, you can easily navigate through your book in a variety of ways:

1. Swipe or Tap to Browse:

- Swipe left or right to flip through pages of the book.
- As you swipe through the pages, you'll see a preview of the next or previous pages in the mini thumbnails at the bottom of the screen.
- Tap on a thumbnail to jump directly to that page. This makes it easy to quickly browse different parts of the book without having to scroll through every page.

2. Move Between Chapters: You can also use Page Flip to quickly navigate between chapters. When you swipe, the Kindle Paperwhite will take you through the pages of the current chapter, but you can also easily skip ahead to the next chapter by swiping to the end of the chapter. The thumbnails will update as you move, giving you a clear view of where you are in the book.

3. Find Specific Pages: If you want to go directly to a specific location in the book, you can tap on the **Go To** button at the top of the screen and choose the page or chapter you wish to skip to. Once you're in the desired section, you can continue flipping through pages with the Page Flip feature.

Features of Page Flip

1. Mini-Preview: One of the main advantages of Page Flip is the mini-preview at the bottom of the screen. These small thumbnails allow you to see where you are in the book and quickly find your way around. They offer a visual representation of the pages you're flipping through, making it easier to scan content without having to commit to full pages.

2. Keeping Your Place: When using Page Flip, your current location is marked with a small indicator, allowing you to seamlessly jump back to where you left off after browsing other parts of the book. This ensures that you never lose your place, even if you're flipping through multiple pages or chapters.

3. Zoom In on Text: If you're looking at a page preview and need to read smaller text, you can **zoom in** on the mini-thumbnails for a clearer view. This makes it easier to get the context of the text before deciding to return to your current reading location.

Benefits of Kindle Page Flip

- **Efficient Navigation**: Page Flip helps you navigate through long books, non-fiction works, and textbooks with ease, without needing to swipe back and forth or search for specific pages manually.

- **Compare Text**: If you need to compare a passage or figure out a reference, Page Flip lets you view multiple pages at once without losing your current position, making it perfect for reading and studying.
- **Time-saving**: Instead of flipping back and forth to find a particular section, Page Flip allows you to jump directly between parts of the text, saving you time and effort.
- **No Interruptions to Your Reading**: One of the best things about Page Flip is that it doesn't disrupt your reading experience. You can quickly jump between sections and return to where you left off without any frustration.

Deactivating Page Flip

Once you're done using Page Flip, simply tap the **back arrow** or **exit button** to disable it and return to your normal reading view. The Kindle Paperwhite will return to its regular page-turning mode, and you can resume reading without the mini-thumbnails at the bottom.

Navigating with the "Go To" Button

The **"Go To" button** is an incredibly useful feature on the Kindle Paperwhite, designed to help you quickly navigate to a specific location, chapter, or section of a book without having to swipe through multiple pages. Whether you're looking for a particular chapter, a bookmarked page, or even a specific location within the text, the "Go To" button streamlines the process, making it easy and efficient to jump exactly where you want to be. Here's how to make the most of this navigation tool.

How to Access the "Go To" Button

To use the **Go To** feature, follow these simple steps:

1. Open a Book: Start by opening the book you wish to navigate.

2. Tap the Top of the Screen: Tap on the top of the screen to bring up the **toolbar**.

3. Select the "Go To" Button: In the toolbar, you'll see a button labeled **"Go To"**. Tap this to access various navigation options.

Navigating with "Go To"

Once you tap the "Go To" button, you'll be presented with several options to help you navigate directly to a specific part of the book. These options include:

1. Table of Contents: For books that have a **Table of Contents** (such as novels or textbooks), you can tap on this option to view the full list of chapters and sections. From here, you can jump directly to the start of any chapter or section. The Kindle will display a list of chapter titles and allow you to tap on the one you want to read.

2. Location: If you know the specific location or position you want to jump to, you can enter the **location number** directly. Each page or section in a Kindle book has a unique location number (which is different from a traditional page number). To use this feature:

- Tap on the **Location** field.
- Enter the specific **location number** or type a rough idea of where you'd like to go (for instance, entering "25%" will take you to approximately the 25% mark of the book).
- Tap **Go To** to navigate to that exact point.

3. Bookmarks: If you've marked certain pages or passages as **bookmarks**, you can access all of them directly through the "Go To" menu. This is particularly helpful when you want to revisit specific points in a book, such as key scenes in a novel or important passages in a reference book. Just tap on **Bookmarks** to see a list of all your saved pages, and then tap on the one you wish to return to.

4. Notes & Highlights: If you've highlighted passages or made notes while reading, you can easily navigate to them using the "Go To" button. By tapping on **Your Notes and Highlights**, you can see all the highlights and annotations you've made throughout the book. This feature is great for reviewing important concepts, quotes, or passages you might want to revisit later.

5. Search: Another option within the "Go To" button is **Search**. If you're looking for a specific word, phrase, or topic, you can type it in and navigate directly to any instance of that term within the book. This makes it easier than ever to find a specific reference or idea without having to scroll or flip through pages.

6. End of Book: If you want to quickly navigate to the end of the book to see the final page or chapter, you can select the **End** option from the "Go To" menu. This is especially useful if you're checking out the conclusion of a book, an afterword, or other end-of-book materials such as an author's note or index.

Advanced Navigation Options ·

In addition to the standard features of the "Go To" button, there are some advanced options that can further enhance your navigation experience:

- **Jump to a Percentage**: Instead of using location numbers, you can jump to a specific **percentage** of the book's progress. For instance, if you're in the middle of a long book and want to go to the 50% mark, simply type "50%" in the location bar and the Kindle Paperwhite will take you there.
- **Page Numbers (in Supported Books)**: For books that use traditional pagination, you can also navigate by **page numbers**. If you prefer to use page numbers instead of locations, you can select this option in the Kindle Paperwhite's settings (under **Reading Options**) and navigate by page number.

Why Use the "Go To" Button?

The "Go To" feature is a time-saver, providing a way to **jump directly** to the content that interests you most. Here are some benefits of using the "Go To" button:

1. Quick Access to Specific Sections: Rather than swiping through multiple pages or chapters, you can directly jump to the content you want to read, making it much easier to explore particular sections or review your highlights.

2. Efficient for Study and Research: The "Go To" button is especially useful for reference books, textbooks, or any non-fiction work where you may need to look up information or revisit important sections. By using the **Search**, **Notes**, and **Highlights** options, you can efficiently move between important sections without having to manually scroll or search for them.

3. Better Organization: If you're reading a book with a complex structure or many chapters, the **Table of Contents** feature in the "Go To" button helps you navigate easily, even if you're reading a book in a non-linear fashion.

4. Quick Navigation for Re-reading: If you're going back to re-read a specific part of a book, whether it's a memorable scene, a key piece of dialogue, or a pivotal moment, the "Go To" feature allows you to find exactly where you left off without wasting time.

Chapter 5

Enhancing Your Reading Experience

Adjusting Font, Brightness, and Themes

One of the standout features of the Kindle Paperwhite is its **customizability**, allowing you to adjust the font, brightness, and themes to suit your personal reading preferences. Whether you're reading in bright sunlight or dim lighting, or if you have specific font and theme preferences, these settings ensure that your reading experience is as comfortable as possible.

Adjusting Font Style and Size

The Kindle Paperwhite gives you full control over the **font style** and **font size**, allowing you to tailor the text to your liking. This is especially beneficial for readers who have visual preferences or specific reading habits.

- **Changing Font Style**: To change the font style, tap the top of the screen while reading to bring up the toolbar. From there, tap the **Aa** icon, which will open the font and layout options. Here, you can choose from a variety of fonts, including options designed for readability like **Bookerly** and **Amazon Ember**. Each font is designed to offer an optimal reading experience, and you can easily switch between them based on your personal preference.

- **Adjusting Font Size**: Within the same **Aa** menu, you can adjust the **font size** by sliding the scale from smaller to larger. Whether you prefer a more compact text for longer reading sessions or larger text for ease of reading, this feature ensures that the font fits your needs. Larger fonts are especially useful for readers with visual impairments or anyone who prefers less strain on their eyes.

- **Changing Line Spacing and Margins**: In addition to adjusting font size and style, the Kindle Paperwhite allows you to modify the **line spacing** and **margins**. You can choose from several options, such as tighter or more spacious lines, and adjust the width of the margins to suit your reading preference. This ensures that the text appears just the way you like it, making it easier and more comfortable to read for long periods.

Adjusting Brightness

One of the key features of the Kindle Paperwhite is its **built-in front light**, which allows you to read comfortably in any lighting condition. Whether you're outdoors on a sunny day or in a dimly lit room, you can adjust the brightness to suit your environment.

- **Automatic Brightness Adjustment**: The Kindle Paperwhite features **adaptive brightness**, which automatically adjusts the screen brightness based on the ambient light around you. This ensures that the screen remains readable without straining your eyes. However, if you prefer more control, you can disable this feature and manually adjust the brightness.
- **Manual Brightness Control**: To adjust the brightness manually, simply tap the top of the screen to bring up the toolbar. In the toolbar, you'll find a **brightness icon** (a sun symbol) that allows you to slide the brightness control up or down. Increase the brightness for well-lit environments, or decrease it for reading at night or in darker surroundings. The Kindle Paperwhite also ensures that the brightness is even across the

screen, providing a consistent reading experience without any hotspots or glare.

Choosing a Theme

The Kindle Paperwhite offers customizable **themes** to further enhance your reading comfort. These themes change the background and text colors to suit different lighting conditions or your personal preferences.

- **Light Mode**: The default setting is **Light Mode**, which features black text on a white background. This is ideal for bright environments, such as outdoor reading or reading during the day. It's crisp, clear, and familiar for most readers.
- **Dark Mode**: For reading at night or in low-light conditions, **Dark Mode** reverses the color scheme, with white text on a black background. This mode reduces the strain on your eyes and can make reading more comfortable in dim environments. It also helps save battery life when the front light is dimmed.
- **Customizing Themes**: To switch between these themes, simply tap the **Aa** icon while reading to access the font and layout settings. From there, you can toggle between Light and Dark Mode, depending on your preference. You can also adjust the font size and line spacing for each

theme, allowing you to create the perfect reading setup.

Other Display Features

Beyond the font, brightness, and theme adjustments, the Kindle Paperwhite offers a few additional display options that can enhance your reading experience:

- **Orientation Lock**: The Kindle Paperwhite automatically adjusts the screen orientation from **portrait to landscape** when you rotate the device. If you prefer to keep the orientation locked in one position, you can turn off the auto-rotation in the settings, preventing the screen from shifting when you change the position of the device.

- **Page Refresh**: The Kindle Paperwhite also allows you to adjust the **page refresh rate**, which ensures that the text and images on the screen remain sharp and clear. You can set the device to refresh the page every time you turn it, or allow it to refresh less frequently, depending on your preference. This is particularly useful for readers who want to avoid any ghosting (faint marks left behind from previous pages).

Using Vocabulary Builder and Word Wise

The Kindle Paperwhite is not just an e-reader; it's a powerful tool for improving your vocabulary and enhancing your reading experience. Two notable features that support this are **Vocabulary Builder** and **Word Wise**. These features make it easier to understand and remember new words while you read, helping to expand your language skills without interrupting your flow.

Vocabulary Builder

The **Vocabulary Builder** feature on the Kindle Paperwhite allows you to create a personalized dictionary of words that you've looked up while reading. This tool helps you not only discover new words but also revisit them for better retention and understanding. Here's how to make the most of this feature:

- **Automatic Tracking**: Every time you look up a word in the Kindle Paperwhite's dictionary, that word is automatically added to the **Vocabulary Builder**. This is particularly useful if you come across unfamiliar words or technical terms while reading. Instead of having to remember or re-look up the word later, Vocabulary Builder keeps a record for you.

- **Reviewing and Learning**: To access your Vocabulary Builder, tap the **Menu** button and select **Vocabulary Builder**. You'll see a list of words you've looked up, along with their definitions. The feature also lets you quiz yourself on these words by showing the word and then hiding the definition. You can tap on the word to reveal the meaning, helping reinforce the vocabulary in your memory. This makes learning more interactive and helps improve your vocabulary retention over time.

- **Spaced Repetition**: To help you retain these new words, the Vocabulary Builder uses a technique called **spaced repetition**. This method repeats words you've learned at intervals, gradually increasing the time between reviews. The idea is to help transfer the word from short-term memory to long-term memory, improving your ability to recall and use the word in different contexts.

- **Integration with Kindle**: Vocabulary Builder is fully integrated with your Kindle experience, so all you need to do is look up words while reading, and the feature will automatically add them to your vocabulary list. This seamless integration ensures that you can focus on reading without interrupting your progress.

Word Wise

Word Wise is another feature that helps you improve your understanding of a book's language. It's particularly useful for readers who are tackling books with complex vocabulary or who are learning a new language. Word Wise provides simple definitions or explanations for difficult words directly above the text as you read.

- **How It Works**: When you turn on Word Wise, short and simple **definitions or synonyms** for difficult words appear above the text. These definitions are concise and easy to understand, providing just enough context to help you comprehend the word without breaking your reading flow. For example, if you come across a word like "ephemeral," a brief definition like "lasting for a very short time" may appear above it.

- **Customizable Difficulty**: Word Wise gives you control over the level of help you want. You can toggle Word Wise on or off, and if you prefer a simpler or more detailed explanation, you can adjust the level of difficulty. In the **Settings** menu, you'll find options to adjust the frequency of definitions or make them more complex depending on your needs.

- **Works for Multiple Languages**: Word Wise isn't just useful for books in English; it also supports several other languages, including Spanish, French, German, Italian, and more. If you're reading a book in a foreign language or learning a new language, Word Wise can offer instant translations or simplified explanations, making it easier to understand unfamiliar words.
- **Enhanced Reading Flow**: One of the best aspects of Word Wise is that it doesn't interrupt the flow of reading. Definitions appear in small, non-intrusive text just above the word, allowing you to keep your eyes on the page while still getting the information you need. This minimizes disruptions and helps you stay immersed in the book.
- **How to Activate Word Wise**: To enable Word Wise, simply go to the **Settings** menu, choose **Reading Options**, and toggle the **Word Wise** setting on or off. You can also customize the difficulty of the explanations by adjusting the level of assistance you receive.

Combining Both Features for Maximum Benefit

When used together, **Vocabulary Builder** and **Word Wise** can significantly improve your understanding and retention of new vocabulary. As you read, Word Wise offers immediate definitions for difficult words, allowing you to keep reading without losing momentum. Then, by adding those words to your **Vocabulary Builder**, you can review and reinforce them later, improving your vocabulary over time.

Additionally, since both features are integrated seamlessly into the Kindle Paperwhite, they don't interfere with your reading experience. You can focus on enjoying your book while effortlessly building your vocabulary.

Highlighting, Notes, and Bookmarks

The Kindle Paperwhite is designed to make your reading experience not only enjoyable but also interactive and productive. One of the most powerful features of the Kindle Paperwhite is the ability to **highlight text**, **make notes**, and **bookmark pages**. These features are especially useful for readers who want to engage with the material, whether for personal reflection, study, or reference. Here's a detailed look at how to use these tools effectively:

Highlighting Text

Highlighting is one of the simplest ways to mark important sections of a book that you may want to revisit later. Whether you're reading for leisure or studying, highlighting helps you easily capture key ideas, quotes, or passages.

- **How to Highlight**: To highlight text on your Kindle Paperwhite, simply tap and hold on the first word of the passage you want to highlight, then drag your finger across the screen to select the desired text. Once the text is selected, a **highlight** option will appear in the toolbar. Tap on the "Highlight" button, and the text will be marked.
- **Multiple Highlights**: You can highlight multiple sections of a book, and each highlighted passage will appear as a distinct block of text. This makes it easy to refer back to all the places you found noteworthy in your book. The Kindle also stores all of your highlights in one place, allowing you to review them later.

- **Sharing Highlights**: After highlighting, you can share your selections with others. You can send a highlighted passage via email, share it on social media, or even add it to your Kindle Notes section. This feature is particularly useful for sharing your favorite quotes or passages from a book with friends or colleagues.

Making Notes

In addition to highlighting, the Kindle Paperwhite allows you to make **notes** on specific parts of a book. This is especially beneficial for deeper engagement with the text, whether for reflection, analysis, or remembering personal thoughts.

- **How to Make Notes**: To add a note, tap and hold on a word or section of text you want to comment on, then select **Note** from the menu that pops up. A text box will appear where you can type your thoughts, observations, or questions. Once finished, tap **Save**, and your note will be attached to that highlighted section.
- **Notes**: All of your notes are stored together in the **Notes and Highlights** section, which can be accessed through the main menu. This feature is ideal for students or professionals who need to organize key information from their reading for later review. You can easily navigate to any

section in the book where you've added a note and continue your study or review process.

- **Exporting Notes**: If you want to save or share your notes outside of the Kindle ecosystem, you can export them to your email or save them in a document format. This makes it simple to keep track of key insights, quotes, or ideas from multiple books without needing to manually transcribe them.

Adding Bookmarks

Bookmarks are a great way to mark pages or sections that you want to quickly return to later. Whether you want to mark a favorite chapter, an important piece of information, or simply save your place, bookmarks offer a simple solution.

- **How to Add a Bookmark**: To add a bookmark, simply tap the top of the screen to bring up the toolbar. Then, tap the **bookmark icon** (a ribbon-shaped symbol) at the top right corner. This will place a bookmark on the current page, which can easily be accessed later.
- **Accessing Bookmarks**: To view your bookmarks, tap the **Menu** icon and select **Go to**. Under this option, you'll find the **Bookmarks** section, where all the pages you've marked are listed. You can tap on any of the bookmarks to

return to that page directly, saving time and effort in finding key sections.

- **Removing Bookmarks**: If you no longer need a bookmark, you can easily remove it. Just go back to the page with the bookmark, tap the **bookmark icon** again, and it will be removed.

Combining Highlights, Notes, and Bookmarks

The true power of the Kindle Paperwhite comes from its ability to combine **highlights**, **notes**, and **bookmarks** to create a personalized study or reading experience.

- **Organizing Content**: When you read a book with several important sections, combining these features allows you to capture and organize key ideas, quotes, and notes all in one place. You can highlight an important passage, add a note for deeper thoughts, and then bookmark the page for easy reference later. This creates a comprehensive record of your reading experience, which is especially valuable for studying or analyzing a book.
- **Reviewing and Reflecting**: By accessing the **Notes and Highlights** section, you can review all your annotations in one place. This is ideal for anyone who wants to quickly revisit key points or reflect on how a book has impacted them. If you're using Kindle Paperwhite for studying, this

function allows you to go back to all the important pieces of information in just a few taps.

Tips for Efficient Use of Highlights, Notes, and Bookmarks

- **Use color-coded or tagged highlights**: If you prefer to highlight different types of information (e.g., key facts, quotes, ideas), consider assigning specific colors to each type of highlight. This isn't a feature currently available on Kindle Paperwhite, but you can use **Notes** to mark your highlights with a specific tag or note about the type of information.

- **Organize by themes**: If you are reading a non-fiction book or academic text, it's helpful to create a system where you highlight themes or specific topics. For example, you could highlight key arguments, supporting data, or quotes, and then add notes to further elaborate on your thoughts.

- **Make use of the search function**: When reviewing your highlights and notes, the **search function** on the Kindle Paperwhite can help you quickly find specific words or topics that you've marked. This makes it easier to locate important ideas or themes, especially if you've accumulated many highlights.

Chapter 6

Advanced Features

The Kindle Paperwhite is designed to cater to a wide variety of users, making it easy to share the device among family members, friends, or colleagues. One of the key features for multi-user households or shared devices is the ability to add **multiple accounts**. This allows each user to access their own library, content, and personalized settings without interfering with other users' experiences. Here's a step-by-step guide on how to add and manage multiple accounts on your Kindle Paperwhite.

Understanding the Benefits of Multiple Accounts

Adding multiple accounts to your Kindle Paperwhite offers several advantages:

- **Personalized Libraries**: Each account can have its own collection of books, audiobooks, and other content. This prevents your content from being mixed up with someone else's, making it easy to find and organize your personal library.
- **Syncing Content**: When multiple accounts are added, each account can sync with its own Amazon account. This ensures that your reading progress, notes, and highlights are saved separately for each user, allowing everyone to pick up right where they left off.
- **Family Sharing**: With multiple accounts, you can set up a shared library or use features like **Amazon Household** to share books across accounts. This is ideal for families who want to share books without purchasing them multiple times.

Adding Multiple Accounts to Your Kindle Paperwhite

Here's how you can add and manage multiple accounts on your Kindle Paperwhite:

Step 1: Open Settings

1. **Turn on your Kindle Paperwhite** by pressing and holding the power button.

2. Tap the **Menu icon** (three horizontal lines) at the top of the screen.

3. Select **Settings** from the drop-down menu.

Step 2: Add Another Account

1. In the **Settings** menu, select **My Account**.

2. Tap **Deregister Device** if the current account is already set up, as you need to deregister it before you can add a new account. (Don't worry, this won't erase your content; it just removes the association with the current account.)

3. After deregistering, you will be prompted to register a new account. Tap **Sign In** or **Create Account** to either sign in with another Amazon account or set up a new one.

- If you're creating a new account, follow the on-screen instructions to set up an Amazon account.
- If you want to add an additional user without deregistering your current account, you can create an **Amazon Household**, which allows you

to share Kindle content without logging out of your primary account.

Step 3: Using Amazon Household for Shared Libraries

If you want to share books between multiple users without switching accounts constantly, Amazon offers the **Amazon Household** feature. This allows two adults and up to four children to share their Kindle libraries and manage parental controls. Here's how you can set it up:

1. **Navigate to Amazon's Website**: You will need to log in to your **Amazon account** through a web browser.

2. Go to **Account & Lists** and select **Your Content and Devices**.

3. Under the **Preferences** tab, scroll down to **Amazon Household** and select **Add Adult** or **Add a Child**.

4. Follow the prompts to link accounts and share books between the users.

Step 4: Switching Between Accounts

After adding multiple accounts, you can switch between them without logging in and out every time:

1. Go to the **Settings** menu on your Kindle.

2. Select **My Account**, and you will see a list of registered accounts.

3. Select the account you want to switch to and tap **Switch Account**. Your Kindle will automatically sync the content associated with that account.

Managing Multiple Accounts and Content

Once multiple accounts are added to the Kindle Paperwhite, it's important to know how to manage the content associated with each one.

- **Content Management**: Each account's content (books, audiobooks, etc.) will be organized separately. You can access the content from the **Home Screen**, where the Kindle Paperwhite will display your content from each account in a distinct section.
- **Syncing Content**: Your content, such as reading progress, bookmarks, and notes, will sync with the correct account when you switch between users. Each account will save its own reading data separately.
- **Parental Controls**: If you've set up an Amazon Household with children, you can manage **parental controls** to restrict access to certain types of content. For example, you can set filters for books and audiobooks suitable for

children, ensuring that your Kindle Paperwhite is kid-friendly.

Deleting an Account

If you need to remove an account from your Kindle Paperwhite, follow these steps:

1. Go to the **Settings** menu.

2. Tap **My Account**, then select **Deregister** next to the account you wish to remove.

3. Confirm the action, and the account will be removed from the device. If you want to switch to a different account, you can follow the steps to sign in again.

Understanding Device and Cloud Storage

The Kindle Paperwhite offers a seamless reading experience by integrating both **device storage** and **cloud storage**. These two storage options work together to ensure you can access your content anytime, anywhere, while maintaining a well-organized library. Whether you prefer to store books locally on your device or in the cloud, understanding the difference between these storage types and how to manage them is key to optimizing your Kindle Paperwhite.

Device Storage

Device storage refers to the physical memory built into your Kindle Paperwhite where you can store eBooks, audiobooks, PDFs, and other content directly on the device. The amount of storage available on the Kindle Paperwhite varies by model, but typically it offers between **8GB and 32GB** of storage.

How Device Storage Works:

- **Local Storage**: When you download content directly to your Kindle Paperwhite, it is stored in the device's internal memory. This includes purchased eBooks, audiobooks, and personal documents (like PDFs) that you transfer from your computer.
- **Reading Experience**: All content stored on your Kindle Paperwhite is available for offline reading, which is ideal for users who may not have constant internet access. If you're going on a trip or traveling to an area with limited connectivity, you can ensure that your favorite books are readily available.
- **Space Management**: You can store thousands of books in the device's internal memory, with the

number depending on the file sizes of your content. Audiobooks, for example, tend to take up more space than regular eBooks.

Managing Device Storage:

- To check the available storage on your Kindle Paperwhite, go to **Settings**, then select **Device Options**, and tap on **Device Info**. Here, you can see how much storage is in use and how much is free.
- **Deleting Content**: If you run out of space or want to remove content you no longer need, you can delete eBooks or documents directly from your device. Just tap and hold the book cover, and choose **Remove from Device**. This will delete the content from your Kindle while keeping it available in your cloud storage for future downloads.

Cloud Storage

Cloud storage refers to the virtual storage available through Amazon's cloud services, which allows you to store and access your Kindle content remotely. The **Amazon Cloud** offers virtually unlimited storage for all your Kindle books, which means you don't have to worry about running out of space for eBooks.

How Cloud Storage Works:

- **Amazon Library**: Every time you purchase or download a Kindle book, it is automatically stored in the Amazon cloud. This includes any content you've purchased from the Kindle Store, as well as personal documents you've sent to your Kindle email address (such as PDFs, Word documents, etc.).
- **Syncing and Access**: Content stored in the cloud is always available for download to your Kindle Paperwhite, as long as you have an internet connection. This means you can download your books onto any Kindle device or app associated with your Amazon account.
- **Backup and Retrieval**: Cloud storage acts as a backup for your Kindle content. If you ever lose or damage your Kindle Paperwhite, you can easily restore your library by signing into your Amazon account on a new device. Similarly, you can download any book you previously purchased or archived.

Managing Cloud Storage:

- **Accessing Your Cloud Library**: Your entire cloud library is available through the **Cloud** section of your Kindle Paperwhite. To view the cloud-based content, tap on **All** on the home screen to see both your device and cloud collections.

- **Archiving Content**: If you have limited device storage and want to free up space, you can **archive** eBooks to the cloud. Archiving removes the book from your Kindle Paperwhite, but it remains available in your cloud library for re-download whenever you want.

- **Downloading from Cloud**: To download a book from the cloud, simply tap on the title in your library, and it will begin downloading to your device. Once downloaded, the book will be available for offline reading.

Device vs. Cloud: Key Differences

Storage Capacity:

- **Device Storage**: Limited by the available memory on your Kindle Paperwhite (8GB or 32GB).

- **Cloud Storage**: Virtually unlimited for eBooks purchased from Amazon, with no physical limitations.

Access to Content:

- **Device Storage**: Once content is downloaded to your Kindle, it is available offline.

- **Cloud Storage**: Content in the cloud requires an internet connection to download to your device.

Syncing:

- **Device Storage**: Syncs your content across all devices registered to your account (e.g., Kindle, Kindle app on smartphones, tablets).
- **Cloud Storage**: Keeps your content in sync with your Amazon account, allowing access from any device.

Tips for Efficient Storage Management

- **Regularly Archive Unused Books**: If you prefer to keep your device's storage tidy, archive books that you're not currently reading. This will free up space while keeping them easily accessible in your cloud library.
- **Monitor Storage Usage**: Regularly check how much space is being used on your Kindle Paperwhite. This can help you determine if you need to offload content to the cloud or delete unnecessary files.
- **Use Collections**: Organize your eBooks into Collections on both your device and cloud. This makes it easier to find your books, whether they are stored locally on your device or in the cloud.

- **Offline Reading**: If you want to read without worrying about an internet connection, download books in advance, especially if you plan to travel or visit areas with poor connectivity.

Troubleshooting Storage Issues

- **Low Storage Warning**: If your device is running out of space, it may prompt you with a warning. You can manage this by deleting unneeded books, archiving older content, or transferring files to another device.
- **Books Not Downloading**: If you are having trouble downloading content from the cloud, make sure you have an active Wi-Fi connection. If the issue persists, try restarting your Kindle Paperwhite or ensuring that your Amazon account is properly linked to your device.
- **Unable to Remove Content**: If you're unable to delete content from your Kindle, ensure that the book isn't currently in use (i.e., being read or playing audio). Sometimes, a quick restart of the device resolves such issues.

Managing Your Kindle Content

One of the standout features of the Kindle Paperwhite is its ability to seamlessly manage your eBooks, audiobooks, PDFs, and other digital content. Whether you are an avid reader, a casual book lover, or someone who uses Kindle for both work and leisure, understanding how to manage your content is essential for an organized and enjoyable reading experience. Here's a comprehensive guide on how to effectively manage your Kindle content.

Organizing Your Content

The Kindle Paperwhite makes it easy to organize your content into different sections for easy access. This is especially useful if you have a large library and want to categorize your books or other materials.

Creating Collections:

Collections are folders that allow you to group similar content together, making it easier to navigate your library. For example, you could create collections for **fiction**, **non-fiction**, **work-related**, or even **current reads**. Here's how to create and manage collections on your Kindle Paperwhite:

1. Go to Your Home Screen: Tap on the **Home** icon.

2. Tap the Menu Button (three horizontal lines) at the top of the screen.

3. Select **Create New Collection**.

4. Enter a name for your collection (e.g., "Mystery Novels").

5. **Add Books**: You can then add books to this collection by selecting them from your library.

Once you've created your collections, they will appear on your home screen, making it easy to access related content.

Archiving Content

To keep your device organized and free up space, you can archive books you're not currently reading. Archiving content removes it from your device but retains it in the cloud, so you can always re-download it when needed.

Archiving Content:

1. **Go to the Home Screen** and locate the content you want to archive.

2. Tap and hold the title of the book.

3. Select **Archive** from the menu options. The book will be removed from your device but will remain available in the cloud.

When you need the content again, you can easily download it from the cloud by tapping on the book cover.

Deleting Content

Sometimes, you may want to permanently remove content from your Kindle Paperwhite, such as books you've already read or items you no longer need. Deleting content removes it from your device and your Amazon account, ensuring you no longer have access to it.

Deleting Content:

1. **Go to the Home Screen** and tap and hold the book you want to delete.

2. Select **Delete from Library** or **Remove from Device**.

- **Delete from Library**: This option removes the book from both your device and your Amazon account, meaning you'll need to repurchase it if you want it again.
- **Remove from Device**: This removes the book from your Kindle, but it will remain in your

cloud library, allowing you to re-download it anytime.

Managing Books Across Devices

One of the benefits of having a Kindle account is that your books are synced across all devices that are linked to the same Amazon account. This means you can start reading on your Kindle Paperwhite and pick up right where you left off on your Kindle app, smartphone, or tablet.

Syncing Content:

- Ensure that **Whispersync** is turned on to sync your reading progress, bookmarks, highlights, and notes across all your devices. To enable Whispersync:

1. Go to **Settings**.

2. Select **Device Options**.

3. Turn on **Whispersync for Books**.

If you're not seeing a book you've purchased on your Kindle Paperwhite, ensure your devices are synced. You can manually sync your Kindle by tapping **Settings** > **Sync My Kindle**.

Using the Kindle Cloud

The Kindle Cloud is a virtual storage space where all of your Amazon-purchased books and documents are stored, even after you've removed them from your device. This ensures you never lose access to your purchased content, no matter how much space you need on your Kindle Paperwhite.

Accessing Cloud Content:

To access your cloud content:

1. From the Home Screen, tap on **All** to view all books stored in both your device and cloud.

2. Books that are stored in the cloud but not downloaded to your device will be marked with a cloud icon. Simply tap on the book to download it to your Kindle Paperwhite.

Managing Personal Documents

In addition to books from the Kindle Store, you can also send personal documents, such as PDFs and Word files, to your Kindle Paperwhite. These documents can be sent to your Kindle email address or manually transferred via USB.

Sending Documents to Your Kindle:

1. Each Kindle device has a unique email address (e.g., yourname@kindle.com).

2. You can send personal documents directly to this email from your computer or phone.

3. Once sent, the documents will appear in your library under **Docs**.

4. Personal documents can also be archived in the cloud or removed from your device to save space.

Managing Subscriptions

If you have Kindle Unlimited or have subscribed to Kindle's periodicals (such as magazines or newspapers), managing these subscriptions is essential to avoid unnecessary charges and ensure you're always up-to-date with the latest issues.

Managing Kindle Unlimited:

- Go to **Settings** > **Subscription & Content** to manage your Kindle Unlimited subscription and the books you've borrowed.
- You can borrow up to 10 books at a time with Kindle Unlimited, and if you reach this limit, you'll need to return one before borrowing another.

Managing Periodicals:

- Periodicals (magazines, newspapers, etc.) are managed separately in your **Periodicals** section. If you no longer want to receive a subscription, go to the **Amazon website** under **Manage Your Content and Devices**, select the subscription, and cancel it.

Troubleshooting Content Management Issues

At times, you may encounter issues with managing your content, such as books not downloading, syncing issues, or problems with archiving or deleting content. Here are some solutions:

- **Book Not Downloading**: Make sure your Kindle is connected to Wi-Fi, and try syncing your device from the **Settings** menu.
- **Sync Issues**: Ensure **Whispersync** is enabled on your account, and check if your Kindle Paperwhite is connected to the internet.
- **Content Not Showing in Library**: Ensure the content has been properly transferred to your Kindle Paperwhite and that your Amazon account is correctly linked.

Chapter 7

Content Management

Downloading and Deleting Books

Managing your Kindle library effectively is crucial for an enjoyable reading experience. The Kindle Paperwhite offers an intuitive way to download, remove, and manage books, ensuring that you always have access to your favorite reads while also keeping your device's storage optimized. In this section, we'll dive into how to **download** books to your Kindle Paperwhite and **delete** content when you no longer need it.

Downloading Books to Your Kindle Paperwhite

One of the main advantages of the Kindle Paperwhite is its seamless integration with Amazon's vast library of eBooks. Whether you're buying a book, borrowing it through Kindle Unlimited, or receiving a personal document, downloading content to your Kindle is straightforward.

Steps to Download Books:

1. **Browse the Kindle Store**:

- To buy a new book, go to the **Amazon Kindle Store** on your Paperwhite. Tap the **Store** button at the top of your home screen to access the Kindle Store. You can search for books by genre, author, or title.
- You can also purchase books from the **Amazon website** on your computer or mobile device, and they will be delivered directly to your Kindle Paperwhite

2. **Download from the Cloud**: Once you've bought or downloaded a book, it will automatically be stored in your **cloud** library, accessible from your Kindle Paperwhite. To download a book from the cloud:

1. From the home screen, tap **All** to show both content stored on your device and in the cloud.

2. Find the book you want to download. Books stored in the cloud will have a small cloud icon next to them.

3. Tap on the book, and it will begin downloading to your device.

3. **Using Kindle Unlimited**: If you are subscribed to Kindle Unlimited, you can borrow books directly from your Kindle Paperwhite. Simply search for a title available through Kindle Unlimited and tap **Borrow**. The book will automatically download to your device.

4. **Downloading Personal Documents**: If you've sent personal documents to your Kindle Paperwhite via email or USB, they will be available in the **Docs** section. To download, tap on the document and it will appear in your library.

5. **Automatic Syncing**: When you make a purchase on Amazon, the book will be sent to your Kindle Paperwhite automatically. Ensure your Kindle is connected to Wi-Fi for content to sync correctly.

Deleting Books from Your Kindle Paperwhite

While the Kindle Paperwhite's storage is relatively spacious, you may want to delete books you've already read or simply no longer need, either to free up space or organize your library.

Steps to Delete Books from Your Device:

1. **Remove from Device**:

- When you remove a book from your device, it is deleted locally but remains stored in the cloud, so you can always download it again later. Here's how to delete content from your Kindle Paperwhite:

1. From your home screen, find the book you wish to delete.

2. Tap and hold the title of the book until a menu appears.

3. **Select Remove from Device**. This will delete the book from your Kindle, but it will remain in your cloud library.

2. **Delete from Library (Permanent Deletion)**: If you want to delete a book permanently, you can remove it from both your device and Amazon's library, meaning it will no longer be accessible in the cloud:

1. Go to **Manage Your Content and Devices** on the **Amazon website**.

2. Find the book you wish to delete.

3. Select **Delete** from the options to permanently remove it from both your device and cloud.

3. **Deleting Personal Documents**: If you've sent personal documents to your Kindle (such as PDFs or Word files), you can delete them directly from the device:

1. Go to the **Docs** section of your Kindle Paperwhite.

2. Tap and hold the document you wish to delete.

3. Select **Remove from Device** to delete it from your Kindle. The document will remain in your cloud and can be re-downloaded when needed.

4. **Archiving vs. Deleting**:

- If you don't want to permanently delete a book but just want to free up space temporarily, you can archive it to the cloud. Archiving removes the book from your Kindle's device memory while keeping it available in the cloud.
- To archive, tap and hold the title of the book and select **Archive**. The book will still appear in your **Cloud** library, where you can download it again at any time.

Managing Your Kindle Library

To keep your Kindle Paperwhite organized, regularly managing your downloaded and deleted books is key. Consider creating **collections** to organize books you've downloaded, such as:

- Currently Reading
- Finished Books
- Favorites
- To Be Read

This organizational method helps you quickly find the content you need while ensuring your Kindle Paperwhite doesn't become overcrowded with unnecessary books.

Troubleshooting Downloading and Deleting Books

If you run into any issues with downloading or deleting books, here are a few tips:

- Books Not Downloading: Ensure your Kindle Paperwhite is connected to Wi-Fi and try syncing your device by going to **Settings > Sync My Kindle**.
- **Books Not Showing Up in Library**: Ensure that your Amazon account is properly linked to your Kindle and that the book has been successfully

delivered to your device. If necessary, restart the Kindle Paperwhite and check again.

- **Unable to Delete Content**: If a book won't delete, ensure it's not currently in use (being read or played) and try again. A restart may help resolve this issue.

Organizing Your Library with Collections

One of the most useful features of the Kindle Paperwhite is the ability to organize your books, documents, and other content into **collections**. This feature is especially helpful if you have a large library, as it allows you to keep your books categorized and easily accessible. Whether you're an avid reader with thousands of titles, or someone who uses the Kindle for both personal and professional purposes, collections can help you stay organized and find the content you need quickly.

What Are Kindle Collections?

A collection on your Kindle Paperwhite is essentially a **folder** where you can group similar books, documents, and other content. You can create collections based on various criteria, such as genre, author, reading status, or any other organizational system that suits you. For instance, you could have collections for:

- Fiction
- Non-fiction
- Currently Reading
- Favorites
- Work/Study Materials
- Books to Revisit
- Books from Kindle Unlimited

How to Create Collections

Creating collections on your Kindle Paperwhite is simple and can be done directly from the home screen. Here's how to set up your own custom collections:

1. **From the Home Screen**:

- Tap the **Menu** button (three horizontal lines) at the top of the screen.
- Select **Create New Collection**.

2. **Name Your Collection**:

- After selecting **Create New Collection**, you'll be prompted to give your collection a name. You can call it something like "Science Fiction" or "2024 Reading List," depending on your organizational preferences.

- Tap **Done** when you've entered your desired name.

3. **Add Books to Your Collection**:

- After creating your collection, you will be asked to **add books**. You can scroll through your library and select the titles you want to add.
- Tap on each book you want to add to the collection. Once selected, tap **Done**.

4. **Access Your Collections**:

Your newly created collection will appear on the **Home Screen**, listed alongside your other books. You can tap on the collection to view the books it contains.

Managing Your Collections

Once you've created your collections, you can manage them by adding or removing books as needed. Here's how to manage your collections:

Adding Books to an Existing Collection:

1. Go to the **Home Screen** and tap the **Menu** button.

2. Select **Collections** to see a list of your existing collections.

3. Tap the collection you want to add books to.

4. Tap the **Add Books** button to select additional books from your library.

5. After selecting the books, tap **Done** to add them to the collection.

Removing Books from a Collection

1. Open the collection from the **Home Screen**.

2. Tap and hold the title of the book you want to remove.

3. Select **Remove from Collection**.

4. The book will remain in your main library, but it will no longer be part of the collection.

Deleting a Collection

1. If you no longer need a collection, you can delete it.

2. Go to the **Home Screen** and tap **Menu**.

3. Select **Collections** and choose the collection you want to delete.

4. Tap **Delete Collection**. This will remove the collection, but the books inside it will remain in your library.

Tips for Organizing Your Kindle Library

Here are a few tips to help you get the most out of the **collections** feature on your Kindle Paperwhite:

- **Use Collections for Progress Tracking**: Create collections such as **"To Read"**, **"Currently Reading"**, and **"Completed"** to track your progress. This way, you can see what's next on your reading list and easily pick up where you left off.
- **Group by Genre or Author**: If you read a lot of specific genres or authors, creating collections like **"Fantasy"**, **"Self-Help"**, or **"Stephen King Books"** can make it easier to find books that match your current mood.
- **Create a 'Favorites' Collection**: If you have books you frequently return to, or those that you've rated highly, create a **"Favorites"** collection to keep them at your fingertips.
- **Use Collections for Work-Related Materials**: If you use your Kindle for professional purposes (such as reading PDFs, reports, or reference books), consider creating collections for different projects or subjects. For example, **"Marketing Research"**, **"Project X Documents"**, or **"Leadership Readings"** can help you easily access work-related content.

Benefits of Organizing with Collections

The **collections** feature on the Kindle Paperwhite offers several benefits that can enhance your reading experience:

- **Improved Organization**: Collections help keep your library tidy and ensure that you can easily find specific books when you need them. This is especially important for readers who have hundreds of books in their library.
- **Faster Access**: Instead of scrolling through a long list of books to find the one you're looking for, collections allow you to jump directly to the category that contains your book, saving time and effort.
- **Easier Management**: As your library grows, collections make it simple to remove old books, add new ones, and maintain an organized space. You can clean up your library without worrying about losing track of important titles.
- **Customization**: You can tailor the organization of your Kindle Paperwhite's content to suit your reading habits. Whether you want to separate fiction from non-fiction, or create a collection for books you want to read again, the flexibility allows you to stay in control.

Transferring Content from an Old Kindle to Your New One

Upgrading to a new Kindle Paperwhite is an exciting experience, and one of the most important tasks after setting up your new device is transferring your content from the old Kindle. Whether you're moving to a newer model or simply replacing a damaged device, Amazon provides several ways to ensure that all your books, documents, and settings are seamlessly transferred to your new Kindle. Here's a detailed guide on how to transfer content from your old Kindle to your new Kindle Paperwhite.

Method 1: Automatic Sync with Your Amazon Account

The easiest and most seamless way to transfer content is through Amazon's **cloud-based system**. All the content you've purchased or downloaded on your previous Kindle device is tied to your Amazon account, meaning it's automatically available on your new Kindle Paperwhite.

Steps to Sync Content Automatically:

1. **Ensure Both Devices are Registered to the Same Amazon Account**: Your old Kindle and new Kindle Paperwhite must be registered to the same Amazon account. If you haven't done so yet, register your new Kindle by going to **Settings** > **My Account** > **Register** and enter your Amazon login details.

2. **Connect Your New Kindle to Wi-Fi**: To start syncing, ensure your new Kindle Paperwhite is connected to a Wi-Fi network. Go to **Settings** > **Wi-Fi** and connect to your preferred network.

3. **Automatic Sync**: Once your new Kindle is connected to Wi-Fi, Amazon will automatically sync all your purchases, books, and documents that are stored in the cloud. These items will appear in your library, and you can download them to your new Kindle Paperwhite at any time.

4. **Access Content in the Cloud**: From the **Home Screen**, tap **All** to view content that is stored in the cloud but not yet downloaded to your device. You can select any book or document to download directly to your new Kindle.

5. **Sync Manually if Needed**: If for any reason the content doesn't sync automatically, you can manually initiate a sync. Go to **Settings** > **Sync My Kindle** to update your library and ensure all content is transferred.

Method 2: Transfer via Amazon's "Manage Your Content and Devices"

For books and documents that may not sync automatically or for those who prefer a manual method, you can transfer content directly through Amazon's **Manage Your Content and Devices** page.

Steps to Transfer Content via Amazon:

1. **Log In to Your Amazon Account**: On a web browser, go to **Amazon's Manage Your Content and Devices page**. Log in using the same Amazon account that's registered on both your old Kindle and your new Kindle Paperwhite.

2. **Go to the Content Tab**: Under the **Content** tab, you will see a list of all the books, documents, and media associated with your account. Find the items you want to transfer to your new Kindle.

3. **Deliver Content to Your New Kindle**: Select the books or documents you wish to transfer, and then click on **Deliver**. A list of registered devices will appear.

Choose your new Kindle Paperwhite from the list, and the selected content will be sent to your new device.

4. **Download on Your New Kindle**: On your new Kindle Paperwhite, ensure it is connected to Wi-Fi and go to the **Cloud** section of your library. Your transferred content will appear here and can be downloaded directly to your device.

Method 3: Transfer Content Using USB

For those who want to manually transfer personal documents, PDFs, or files that are not purchased through Amazon (such as books from other sources or documents you've sent to your old Kindle), you can transfer them via **USB**.

Steps to Transfer via USB:

1. Connect Your Old Kindle to Your Computer:

- Use a USB cable to connect your old Kindle to your computer. Once connected, your Kindle will appear as an external drive.

2. Locate the Files:

- Open the Kindle drive on your computer and navigate to the **Documents** folder. This is where your books and documents are stored.

3. **Copy Files to Your Computer**:

- Select the files you want to transfer (eBooks, PDFs, personal documents, etc.) and copy them to your computer.

4. **Connect Your New Kindle to the Computer**:

- Disconnect your old Kindle and connect your new Kindle Paperwhite to your computer using the USB cable.

5. **Transfer Files to Your New Kindle**:

- Open the Kindle drive for your new device. Paste the files you copied from the old Kindle into the **Documents** folder of your new Kindle Paperwhite.

6. **Eject and Access Files**:

- Safely eject the Kindle from your computer. When you open your new Kindle, the files should appear in your library, and you can begin reading them.

Method 4: Transfer Personal Documents via Email

Another option for transferring personal documents, such as PDFs, Word files, and other non-Amazon content, is to use the Kindle email address associated with your Amazon account.

Steps to Transfer Documents via Email:

1. Find Your Kindle Email Address:

- To find your Kindle's email address, go to **Settings > My Account > Send-to-Kindle Email**.

2. Send Documents to Your New Kindle:

- From your computer or mobile device, email the documents to your Kindle email address. Ensure the files are in a supported format (PDF, Word, etc.).

3. Access on Your Kindle Paperwhite:

- On your new Kindle, go to **Settings > Sync My Kindle** to receive the emailed content. The documents will appear in your library, ready for reading.

Troubleshooting Transfer Issues

Content Not Syncing: If your books or documents aren't syncing to your new Kindle, try syncing manually through **Settings > Sync My Kindle**. Ensure your

Kindle is connected to Wi-Fi and is registered under the correct Amazon account.

- **Missing Books**: If some books are missing, ensure they are still available in your Amazon library. You may need to manually deliver them using the **Manage Your Content and Devices** page.
- **USB Transfer Issues**: If files aren't transferring via USB, ensure the Kindle is correctly recognized by your computer and that you are copying the files into the **Documents** folder.

Chapter 8

Maintenance and Care

To ensure that your Kindle Paperwhite continues to perform optimally and retains its sleek look, regular cleaning and maintenance are necessary. Kindle Paperwhite is built to be durable, but like any electronic device, proper care will prolong its lifespan, prevent issues, and keep it looking new. This guide will walk you through the essential steps for cleaning and maintaining your Kindle Paperwhite.

Cleaning the Screen

The screen is the most essential part of your Kindle Paperwhite. Since it uses **E Ink** technology, it is different from regular LCD screens, and it can attract dust, fingerprints, and smudges. Keeping the screen clean ensures a crisp, clear reading experience.

Steps to Clean the Screen:

1. **Turn Off the Device**: Always turn off your Kindle Paperwhite before cleaning the screen to avoid accidental taps or changes in settings while cleaning.

2. **Use a Soft, Lint-Free Cloth**: Choose a microfiber cloth or any soft, lint-free cloth that won't scratch the screen. Avoid using paper towels, napkins, or other rough fabrics.

3. **Wipe Gently**: Gently wipe the screen in circular motions to remove any dust or fingerprints. Don't press too hard to avoid damaging the display.

4. **Use a Small Amount of Water if Needed**: If the screen is particularly dirty, slightly dampen the cloth with water. Avoid using any cleaning products, sprays, or harsh chemicals, as they can damage the screen. Always make sure the cloth is just damp and not wet, as too much moisture can seep into the device.

Cleaning the Body of the Kindle

The body of your Kindle Paperwhite can also accumulate dirt, dust, and oils from your hands. Regularly cleaning the body will keep your device looking pristine and ensure that buttons and ports function smoothly.

Steps to Clean the Body:

1. **Use a Dry Cloth**: For regular cleaning, simply use a dry microfiber cloth to wipe down the exterior of the Kindle. Be sure to remove any fingerprints or smudges on the back and sides.

2. **Remove Debris from the Ports**: If there's dust or dirt around the charging port or other openings, gently use a soft brush or compressed air to remove it. Avoid using sharp objects that could damage the device.

3. **Avoid Harsh Chemicals**: Never use abrasive or chemical cleaners on the body of your Kindle. Stick to a dry or slightly dampened cloth to prevent any damage to the surface.

Maintaining Battery Health

The Kindle Paperwhite's battery is designed to last for weeks on a single charge, but maintaining battery health is essential to ensuring its longevity.

Battery Maintenance Tips:

1. **Avoid Overcharging**: While the Kindle Paperwhite is designed to handle continuous charging, it's best not to leave it plugged in for too long once it reaches 100%. If possible, unplug it once the battery is full to avoid unnecessary wear on the battery over time.

2. **Use Battery Saving Features**: To conserve battery life, take advantage of features like turning off Wi-Fi when you're not using it and adjusting the screen brightness.

3. **Fully Drain Occasionally**: It's a good idea to fully drain the battery on occasion (to 0%) and then recharge it to 100%. This helps maintain the battery's efficiency and accuracy in tracking the charge level.

4. **Avoid Extreme Temperatures**: Keep your Kindle away from extremely hot or cold environments, as temperature fluctuations can negatively affect the battery. Try to store your Kindle Paperwhite at room temperature when not in use.

Updating Software Regularly

Amazon frequently releases software updates for Kindle devices, including new features, security improvements, and bug fixes. Keeping your Kindle up to date ensures you have the latest features and the best performance.

Steps to Check for Updates:

1. **Connect to Wi-Fi**: Make sure your Kindle Paperwhite is connected to a Wi-Fi network.

2. **Go to Settings**: Tap the **Menu** icon in the top-right corner of the screen and select **Settings**.

3. **Check for Updates**: Tap **Device Options** > **Advanced Options** > **Update Your Kindle**. If an update is available, follow the on-screen instructions to install it. It's always a good idea to keep your device updated to enjoy the best user experience.

Storage Management and File Cleanup

Over time, your Kindle Paperwhite can accumulate unnecessary files, such as old documents or books you've already read. Managing the content stored on your device ensures better performance and saves storage space.

Steps for Managing Storage:

1. **Delete Unwanted Books**: Regularly go through your library and delete books or documents that you no longer need. This can be done from the **Home Screen** or by selecting **Manage Your Content and Devices** on Amazon's website.

2. **Organize with Collections**: Create collections to organize your books more efficiently. This makes it easier to navigate your library and find what you need without wasting time scrolling through a long list of books.

3. **Move to the Cloud**: If you want to keep books but free up space on your device, move them to the cloud. You can access these books anytime by downloading them from the cloud back to your Kindle.

Handling Your Kindle with Care

Taking proper care of your Kindle Paperwhite ensures that it stays in good condition, both functionally and aesthetically. Simple measures, like using a protective case and handling the device carefully, can prevent scratches, drops, and other damage.

Care Tips:

1. **Use a Case**: A protective case or cover will help safeguard your Kindle from scratches and accidental drops. Many cases are designed specifically for the Kindle Paperwhite, providing a snug fit that protects the device without adding too much bulk.

2. **Avoid Exposure to Water**: While the Kindle Paperwhite is **water-resistant** to some extent, it's still a good idea to avoid exposing it to excessive moisture. Be

mindful when using it near pools, beaches, or in damp conditions.

3. **Keep It Away from Extreme Heat**: Excessive heat can warp or damage your Kindle. Avoid leaving it in hot environments, such as in a car on a sunny day or near a heat source.

Troubleshooting Common Issues

Despite its durability, your Kindle Paperwhite may occasionally experience some issues. Regular maintenance and prompt troubleshooting can help resolve most problems.

Common Kindle Problems and Solutions:

1. **Frozen Screen**: If the screen freezes or becomes unresponsive, try restarting your Kindle by holding the power button for about 20 seconds until it restarts.

2. **Battery Draining Quickly**: If the battery drains too quickly, reduce screen brightness, turn off Wi-Fi when not in use, and check if there are any background apps or processes consuming too much power.

3. **Charging Issues**: If your Kindle is not charging properly, check the charging cable and adapter for damage. You may also want to try a different charging cable or outlet to see if the issue is with the cable or port.

Tips to Minimize Interference

While your Kindle Paperwhite is designed to offer a smooth reading experience, certain external factors can cause interference with its performance. Whether it's from environmental conditions, signal interference, or device-specific issues, it's essential to know how to minimize these disruptions for optimal use. Here are some tips to ensure that you can enjoy a seamless Kindle experience, free from interruptions.

Avoid Magnetic and Electronic Interference

Kindle Paperwhite is a sensitive device, and it can be affected by magnetic fields or strong electronic interference. Certain devices, such as speakers, magnets, or heavy-duty electronics, can disrupt the device's performance, particularly its touch screen.

How to Minimize Interference:

- **Keep Away from Magnets**: Avoid placing your Kindle near magnetic sources, such as fridge magnets or magnetic phone cases, as they can interfere with the device's sensors and touch capabilities.

- **Limit Exposure to Other Electronics**: Keep your Kindle away from other electronics like radios, large speakers, or power tools. These devices can emit electromagnetic waves that interfere with the Kindle's wireless connection and touch functionality.

Optimize Wi-Fi Signal for Better Connectivity

Wi-Fi is essential for syncing your Kindle Paperwhite, downloading books, and accessing cloud storage. If you experience slow downloads or syncing issues, it could be due to a weak or congested Wi-Fi signal.

How to Minimize Wi-Fi Interference:

- **Use a Stable Network**: Ensure you are connected to a stable, high-speed Wi-Fi network. A fluctuating or slow network can cause delays in syncing or downloading content.
- **Minimize Wi-Fi Congestion**: If you share your network with multiple devices, such as computers, smartphones, or gaming consoles, this could cause network congestion. Try to use your Kindle Paperwhite when fewer devices are connected, or use a dedicated Wi-Fi network just for your Kindle.
- **Position Near the Router**: If possible, ensure that your Kindle is close enough to the router for

the strongest signal. Avoid thick walls or obstructions that may reduce signal strength.

- **Disable Wi-Fi When Not in Use**: Turn off Wi-Fi when you don't need it to conserve battery and avoid interference with other processes on your device.

Manage Screen Brightness

The Kindle Paperwhite uses an E Ink screen, which is designed for easy reading in various lighting conditions. However, if the brightness is too high or low, it can cause strain on your eyes and, in rare cases, may interfere with the display's clarity.

How to Minimize Display Interference:

- **Adjust Brightness Appropriately**: Use the adjustable brightness feature to ensure that the screen is not too bright or dim for your reading environment. High brightness settings in dark rooms can cause glare and strain, while low brightness in bright settings can make text hard to read.
- **Use Auto-Brightness**: If your Kindle Paperwhite supports automatic brightness adjustment, enable this feature to have the device adjust to changing lighting conditions automatically, reducing the need for manual adjustments.

Keep Your Kindle in a Protective Case

Though the Kindle Paperwhite is designed to be durable and water-resistant, using a protective case helps reduce exposure to accidental drops, bumps, or scratches that can cause physical interference with the device's functionality.

How to Minimize Physical Interference:

- **Use a Soft, Impact-Resistant Case**: Invest in a protective case that is soft and offers shock absorption. This can help protect the device from accidental drops or impacts that may affect its screen or buttons.
- **Avoid Extreme Pressure on the Screen**: When placing your Kindle in bags or pockets, ensure it's not under heavy pressure, as this can cause screen damage or unresponsiveness to touch gestures.

Minimize Power Interference

Sometimes, power fluctuations or improper charging can lead to performance issues with your Kindle. It's crucial to ensure your device is charged properly and that it's not exposed to power surges or interruptions.

How to Minimize Power Interference:

- **Use a Reliable Charging Adapter**: Always use the charging cable and adapter that came with your Kindle Paperwhite. Avoid using third-party chargers, as they may not provide the correct power output, potentially causing battery or charging issues.

- **Avoid Charging While Using**: If you're reading or using other features of your Kindle while charging, it may generate heat or cause performance lags. To minimize this, avoid heavy usage while charging or disconnect it once the battery is fully charged.

- **Monitor Battery Health**: Overcharging can strain the battery and reduce its lifespan. Make it a habit to unplug your Kindle once it's fully charged to prevent overcharging and prolong battery health.

Keep Software Updated

Amazon regularly releases software updates for Kindle Paperwhite that fix bugs, improve features, and address interference-related issues. Keeping your Kindle updated ensures it performs at its best.

How to Minimize Software-Related Interference:

Enable Automatic Updates: Make sure your Kindle is connected to Wi-Fi and has the automatic update feature enabled. This ensures your device will always have the latest improvements and bug fixes.

Manually Check for Updates: If automatic updates are not enabled, you can manually check for updates by going to **Settings** > **Device Options**> **Advanced Options** > **Update Your Kindle**. Updates may fix bugs that cause interference with functionality.

Minimize Interference from Other Apps and Features

Certain features or apps running on your Kindle Paperwhite may cause system slowdowns or interfere with its performance, especially if you've downloaded large files or stored too many documents.

How to Minimize App and System Interference:

- **Delete Unused Content**: If you have large files or books that you no longer need, delete them from your device to free up space. This ensures smoother operation and faster access to your library.
- **Disable Unnecessary Features**: Features such as Wi-Fi, Bluetooth, or sync can be turned off when

not needed to conserve battery and avoid potential interference. This also reduces the chances of background processes slowing down the device.

Keep Your Kindle in Optimal Environmental Conditions

Extreme temperatures, humidity, and direct sunlight can also interfere with the performance of your Kindle Paperwhite.

How to Minimize Environmental Interference:

- **Avoid Exposure to Direct Sunlight**: While the Kindle Paperwhite is sunlight-readable, prolonged exposure to direct sunlight can cause the screen to overheat and degrade its quality over time.
- **Store in a Cool, Dry Place**: Avoid storing your Kindle in excessively hot or humid environments. These conditions can cause screen discoloration, battery damage, and other functional issues.

Chapter 9

Safety and Compliance

Important Safety Tips for Using Your Device

While the Kindle Paperwhite is a durable and user-friendly device, like any electronic gadget, it's important to take precautions to ensure safe usage. Proper handling, charging, and storage of your device will prevent potential hazards and prolong its lifespan. Here are some essential safety tips for using your Kindle Paperwhite.

1. **Use the Correct Charging Equipment**: Always use the charger and cable provided by Amazon or compatible alternatives that meet Kindle's safety standards. Using third-party chargers that are not specifically designed for Kindle can cause electrical surges, overheating, or even permanent damage to the battery.

Safety Tips for Charging

- **Use the Official Charger**: Only use the charging cable and adapter that came with your Kindle Paperwhite or one from a trusted source.
- **Avoid Overcharging**: While the Kindle is designed to stop charging once it's full, try to unplug it when fully charged to prevent any unnecessary wear on the battery.
- **Charge in Safe Environments**: Always plug your Kindle into a dry, well-ventilated power outlet. Avoid charging near water or in high-humidity areas to prevent any risk of short-circuiting.

2. **Protect Your Kindle from Extreme Temperatures**: Your Kindle Paperwhite should be used and stored within recommended temperature ranges to ensure safe operation. Exposure to extreme temperatures can damage the screen, reduce battery life, or cause malfunction.

Safety Tips for Temperature

- **Avoid Direct Heat**: Do not expose your Kindle to heat sources like radiators, hot cars, or stoves. High temperatures can cause the device to overheat and affect its internal components.

- **Don't Leave in Direct Sunlight**: While the Kindle Paperwhite is designed to be readable in direct sunlight, prolonged exposure can damage the screen and cause it to overheat.
- **Store in a Cool, Dry Place**: Keep your Kindle Paperwhite in a cool, dry environment to prevent it from getting too hot or cold. The recommended operating temperature is between 32°F (0°C) and 95°F (35°C).

3. Keep It Away from Water and Moisture: Though the Kindle Paperwhite is water-resistant (IPX8 rated), it is not fully waterproof. It can withstand brief submersions in water, but prolonged exposure to moisture can cause damage to the device.

Safety Tips for Moisture:

- **Avoid Submersion in Water**: While you can safely use your Kindle in the bath or by the pool for short periods, do not submerge it for long durations, especially in salty or chlorinated water, as this may damage the internal components.
- **Don't Use in Wet Conditions**: Never use your Kindle when your hands are wet, and avoid using it in damp environments like showers or saunas where the risk of moisture exposure is higher.

4. **Keep Your Kindle Safe from Physical Damage**: Physical damage, such as cracks in the screen, scratches, or drops, can impair the Kindle Paperwhite's functionality. Proper care and handling are essential to protect the device from unnecessary wear.

Safety Tips for Physical Protection

- **Use a Case**: Invest in a protective case or cover for your Kindle. This will not only protect it from scratches and bumps but also reduce the chances of damage in case it's accidentally dropped.
- **Don't Overload the Device**: While the Kindle is lightweight, avoid putting too much weight on the device by storing heavy objects in the same bag or pocket. Excessive pressure can cause cracks in the screen or damage the internal structure.
- **Handle with Care**: Always handle your Kindle carefully, especially when moving it from one place to another. Avoid throwing it into bags or onto hard surfaces where it could land on its corners or screen.

5. Keep the Device Out of Reach of Children and Pets: Although the Kindle Paperwhite is a durable device, small children and pets may not understand how to handle it properly, which can lead to accidental damage.

Safety Tips for Children and Pets

- **Supervise Use**: If your child or pet is using your Kindle, always supervise them. Children may be tempted to throw or drop the device, while pets might chew on cables or try to paw at the screen.
- **Store Safely**: When not in use, store your Kindle in a safe, secure location where children and pets cannot reach it. This will prevent accidental drops, bites, or other incidents.

6. Avoid Eye Strain and Discomfort: While Kindle Paperwhite's E Ink screen is easy on the eyes, it's still essential to take breaks during extended reading sessions to prevent eye strain or fatigue.

Safety Tips for Reading Comfort

- **Take Breaks**: Follow the 20-20-20 rule—every 20 minutes, take a 20-second break and look at something 20 feet away. This reduces eye strain and helps your eyes stay relaxed.

- **Adjust Screen Brightness**: If you're reading for long periods, adjust the brightness of the screen to a comfortable level. Too much light can cause glare, while too little light can make reading difficult.
- **Read in a Well-Lit Area**: Though the Kindle Paperwhite has a built-in light, reading in low-light conditions for extended periods can still cause discomfort. Try to read in an area with ambient light for the most comfortable experience.

7. **Maintain Battery Health**: The Kindle Paperwhite's battery is designed to last for weeks on a single charge, but neglecting battery maintenance can lead to shorter battery life and issues with charging.

Safety Tips for Battery Health:

- **Avoid Excessive Charging**: Although the Kindle is designed to handle charging, try to unplug it when the battery is fully charged to prevent overcharging and unnecessary stress on the battery.
- **Don't Use While Charging**: Using your Kindle while it's charging can generate heat and strain the battery. If possible, avoid reading or using apps while your device is plugged in.

- **Monitor Battery Levels**: Keep an eye on your battery levels and charge your Kindle when it's below 20%. This helps maintain the long-term health of the battery.

8. **Use Kindle Features Responsibly**: The Kindle Paperwhite offers a variety of features designed to enhance your reading experience. However, some of these features require careful handling to ensure safe and efficient use.

Safety Tips for Features

- **VoiceView Screen Reader**: If you're using the VoiceView screen reader for accessibility, make sure the device is in a quiet environment to prevent external noise from interfering with audio feedback.
- **Wi-Fi and Bluetooth**: Turn off Wi-Fi and Bluetooth when not in use to conserve battery life and prevent security risks. Avoid connecting your Kindle to public Wi-Fi networks to protect your privacy.
- **Device Updates**: Regularly check for software updates to keep your Kindle secure and running smoothly. Updated software helps to fix bugs, improve performance, and enhance device security.

9. **Troubleshooting and Support**: If you ever experience issues with your Kindle, don't hesitate to reach out for support. Amazon provides a variety of troubleshooting resources to help you solve problems safely without risking damage to the device.

Safety Tips for Troubleshooting

- **Avoid Self-Repair**: If your Kindle is malfunctioning, don't attempt to repair it yourself. Opening the device or attempting unauthorized repairs could void the warranty and cause further damage.
- **Use Official Support Channels**: Reach out to Amazon's customer service for support. They can guide you through troubleshooting steps and offer safe solutions for your Kindle Paperwhite.

Regulatory Information

The Kindle Paperwhite, like all electronic devices, is subject to various regulations and standards to ensure its safe use and compliance with environmental laws. Understanding the regulatory information is essential for users to ensure the device is used within the parameters set by regulatory bodies.

1. **Compliance with FCC Regulations**: The Kindle Paperwhite is in compliance with the Federal Communications Commission (FCC) regulations regarding radio frequency (RF) emissions. This means that the device meets the guidelines for limiting exposure to RF energy as established by the FCC, which is aimed at ensuring that electronic devices do not emit harmful levels of radiation.

- **FCC ID**: You can find the FCC ID for your Kindle Paperwhite in the device's settings or user manual.
- **RF Exposure**: The device has been tested for RF exposure in accordance with the FCC guidelines. Users should not operate the device with the antenna placed directly against the body, and should avoid prolonged close contact during operation, such as carrying it in pockets or tight clothing.

2. **CE Marking (European Union)**: For users in the European Union (EU), the Kindle Paperwhite carries the CE mark, which indicates that it complies with the essential requirements of EU directives for safety, health, and environmental protection. This includes the following:

- **Electromagnetic Compatibility (EMC)**: The Kindle Paperwhite complies with EU EMC directives to ensure that it does not cause harmful interference with other electronic devices.
- **Low Voltage Directive (LVD)**: The Kindle Paperwhite also complies with the EU LVD to ensure that it operates safely within the allowed voltage range, reducing the risk of electric shock or fire.
- **RoHS Compliance**: The Kindle Paperwhite adheres to the EU's Restriction of Hazardous Substances (RoHS) directive, which limits the use of certain hazardous materials in the manufacture of electrical and electronic equipment. This is aimed at reducing environmental impact and health risks.

3. **Battery Safety and Handling**: The Kindle Paperwhite uses a lithium-ion battery, which is subject to various safety standards to ensure that it is safe for use and handling.

- **Battery Safety**: To prevent fire, explosion, or injury, do not expose the device to extreme temperatures or physical damage, and always use the official charger designed for the Kindle Paperwhite.
- **Recycling**: When the battery reaches the end of its useful life, ensure that it is disposed of or

recycled properly in accordance with local environmental regulations. Never dispose of the device or battery in regular household waste.

4. **Environmental Considerations**: The Kindle Paperwhite is designed with sustainability in mind. Amazon takes steps to minimize the environmental impact of its products and packaging.

- **Packaging**: The Kindle Paperwhite's packaging is made from recyclable materials wherever possible, and Amazon is continuously working to reduce its carbon footprint by using more sustainable materials.
- **Energy Efficiency**: The Kindle Paperwhite is built to be energy-efficient, with its E Ink display and adjustable front light that helps conserve power. The device is designed to last for weeks on a single charge, reducing the frequency of charging and its environmental impact.

5. **Health and Safety Warnings**: While the Kindle Paperwhite is generally safe for use, users should still follow certain health and safety guidelines:

- **Eye Safety**: Although the Kindle Paperwhite uses an E Ink display that reduces glare and mimics paper, prolonged reading sessions may still cause eye strain. Users are advised to take breaks regularly to avoid fatigue.

- **Hearing Impairment**: If using VoiceView or any other audio features, ensure that the volume is kept at a safe level to prevent hearing damage.
- **Children and Pets**: Keep the Kindle Paperwhite out of reach of young children and pets, as small parts and accessories could pose a choking hazard. Also, ensure that children do not use the device for extended periods to avoid strain on their eyes.

6. **Wireless Network and Radio Frequency Usage**: The Kindle Paperwhite features Wi-Fi and, in some models, cellular connectivity. These wireless communications are regulated to ensure they operate within safe limits for radio frequency exposure.

- **Wi-Fi Compliance**: The device is compliant with local regulations for Wi-Fi usage and will only operate within designated frequency bands for Wi-Fi networks in each region.
- **Cellular Models**: For cellular versions of the Kindle Paperwhite, the device complies with applicable local laws regarding mobile network usage, including communication protocols and frequency bands authorized in each country.

7. **Warranty and Service Information**: The Kindle Paperwhite comes with a standard warranty that covers manufacturing defects for a specific period. Users are advised to keep their purchase receipt for warranty purposes.

- **Warranty Coverage**: The warranty generally covers defects in materials and workmanship under normal use. It does not cover damage resulting from misuse, unauthorized repairs, or accidents.
- **Service and Repairs**: If your Kindle Paperwhite requires service, it is recommended that you contact Amazon's customer support for guidance. Amazon's authorized repair centers are equipped to provide safe and certified repair services.

8. **Compliance with Local Laws**: The Kindle Paperwhite is intended for use in most regions around the world. However, specific laws and regulations may vary depending on the country or region. Ensure that your device is used in accordance with local laws governing electronic devices, including data protection, wireless communication, and safety regulations.

- **Local Compliance**: Before using your Kindle Paperwhite internationally, verify that the device complies with local regulations regarding wireless communication and device safety. Some countries may have restrictions or require certification for electronic devices.

Chapter 10

Troubleshooting and Support

While the Kindle Paperwhite is known for its reliability and ease of use, like any electronic device, users may encounter occasional issues. Below is a list of common problems faced by Kindle Paperwhite users and their corresponding solutions.

1. Kindle Not Turning On

Issue: The device does not power on, even when you press the power button.

Solution:

- **Charge the Device**: Sometimes, the Kindle Paperwhite may not turn on due to a low or drained battery. Plug it into the charger for at least 30 minutes and then try turning it on again.

- **Reset the Device**: If charging doesn't work, try performing a soft reset. Hold the power button for 40 seconds to force a restart. This will not delete your content but may help fix minor system glitches.
- **Check the Charging Cable**: Ensure that the charger and cable are functioning properly. If the cable or adapter is faulty, try using a different one or charging the Kindle with a known working charger.

2. Frozen or Unresponsive Screen

Issue: The Kindle screen is frozen, and none of the touch controls respond.

Solution:

- **Restart the Kindle**: A simple restart can often solve this issue. Hold the power button for 40 seconds, wait for the Kindle to restart, and check if the issue is resolved.
- **Check for Software Updates**: Ensure that your Kindle is running the latest software. You can go to the settings menu and check for any available updates. Sometimes outdated software can cause performance issues.

3. Wi-Fi Connectivity Issues

Issue: The Kindle Paperwhite is unable to connect to Wi-Fi or keeps disconnecting.

Solution:

- **Restart the Device**: Turn the Kindle off and back on to reset its wireless settings.
- **Forget and Reconnect to Wi-Fi**: Go to the Wi-Fi settings, select your network, and choose "Forget." Then, reconnect by entering the Wi-Fi password again.
- **Check Router Settings**: Ensure that your router is working correctly and that the Kindle is within range. If there are any issues with the router, try restarting it.
- **Switch to a Different Network**: If the problem persists, try connecting to a different Wi-Fi network to see if the issue is with your original network.

4. Kindle Not Syncing Content

Issue: Your Kindle Paperwhite is not syncing with your Amazon account, meaning books or other content are not appearing on the device.

Solution:

- **Check Your Internet Connection**: A weak or unstable connection can prevent syncing. Ensure that your Kindle is connected to a stable Wi-Fi network.
- **Sync Manually**: Go to the settings menu and select "Sync My Kindle" to manually sync your device with your Amazon account.
- **Log Out and Back In**: Try logging out of your Amazon account and then logging back in. This can often fix syncing issues.
- **Check for Software Updates**: Ensure your Kindle's software is up to date, as outdated software can sometimes cause syncing problems.

5. **Poor Battery Life**

Issue: The battery drains too quickly, even with minimal use.

Solution:

- **Adjust Brightness**: Reduce the screen brightness or switch to the "Dark Mode" to conserve battery life.
- **Turn Off Wi-Fi**: If you don't need Wi-Fi, turn it off. The Kindle Paperwhite consumes a lot of battery while connected to a network.

- **Close Background Apps**: If you have other apps or features running, close them to conserve power.
- **Reset to Factory Settings**: If your Kindle's battery continues to drain quickly despite these efforts, performing a factory reset might help. Be sure to back up your content before resetting, as this will erase all data on the device.

6. Screen Glare or Poor Visibility

Issue: The screen is hard to read in certain lighting conditions, such as direct sunlight or low light.

Solution:

- **Adjust Screen Brightness**: Use the brightness control to increase or decrease the light based on your reading environment. The Kindle Paperwhite has an adjustable front light that helps in both bright and dim environments.
- **Use the Built-in Dark Mode**: For easier reading in low light, switch to dark mode, which uses white text on a black background.
- **Screen Protector**: If glare persists, consider using a matte screen protector. This will reduce reflections and improve visibility in bright environments.

7. Kindle Not Charging

Issue: The Kindle Paperwhite doesn't seem to charge when connected to the charger.

Solution:

Check the Charging Cable and Adapter: Make sure the cable and adapter are functioning properly. Try using a different charger to see if the issue persists.

Clean the Charging Port: Dust or dirt in the charging port can prevent the device from charging properly. Use a dry cloth or compressed air to clean the port gently.

Try a Different Power Source: Plug the Kindle into a different power outlet, as the one you are using may be malfunctioning.

Charge in the Off State: If the device is unresponsive, try charging the Kindle while it is turned off.

8. Kindle Paperwhite Not Responding to Touch

Issue: The screen does not register taps or swipes, making it impossible to navigate.

Solution:

- **Clean the Screen**: Dirt, grease, or moisture on the screen can interfere with touch sensitivity. Clean the screen gently with a microfiber cloth.

- **Restart the Device**: If the touchscreen is still unresponsive, perform a restart by holding the power button for 40 seconds to reset the device.
- **Remove the Screen Protector**: If you use a screen protector, it may be interfering with the touchscreen. Try removing it and see if the issue is resolved.

9. Audible Content Issues

Issue: Audible audiobooks are not working, or there is no sound.

Solution:

- **Check Audio Settings**: Make sure the volume is turned up and not muted. You can adjust the volume via the device settings or during audiobook playback.
- **Check Bluetooth Connectivity**: If you're using Bluetooth headphones or speakers, ensure that they are properly connected and within range.
- **Re-download the Audiobook**: If the issue persists, try deleting the audiobook and re-downloading it from your Audible library.

10. Kindle Freezes During Updates

Issue: The Kindle Paperwhite freezes during a software update.

Solution:

- **Wait for the Update to Complete**: If your Kindle is stuck on the update screen, give it time. Sometimes updates take longer than expected.
- **Restart the Device**: If it's been stuck for an extended period, perform a soft reset by holding the power button for 40 seconds. The Kindle should reboot and may complete the update after restarting.
- **Contact Amazon Support**: If the device continues to freeze during updates, contact Amazon customer support for assistance.

Resetting Your Kindle Paperwhite

Resetting your Kindle Paperwhite can be a useful solution for fixing persistent issues, such as unresponsiveness, software glitches, or other problems that cannot be resolved with simple troubleshooting. There are two main types of resets you can perform on the Kindle Paperwhite: a **soft reset** and a **hard reset** (also called a **factory reset**). Each serves a different purpose, and knowing when to use each can help keep your device running smoothly.

1. Soft Reset

A soft reset is essentially a restart of your Kindle Paperwhite. This can help fix minor issues without losing any of your data, such as books, settings, or preferences.

Steps for a Soft Reset:

1. **Press and Hold the Power Button**: Locate the power button on your Kindle Paperwhite, typically on the bottom or the back of the device.

2. **Hold for 40 Seconds**: Press and hold the power button for 40 seconds. After this time, the screen may go black.

3. **Wait for the Kindle to Restart**: Release the power button after 40 seconds. Your Kindle should restart automatically. If it doesn't, press the power button again to turn it on.

A soft reset is helpful if the device is freezing or unresponsive, if it's having trouble syncing, or if there's a minor software issue. It won't delete any of your content, so it's a safe first step before attempting more drastic measures.

2. Hard Reset (Factory Reset)

A factory reset (also known as a hard reset) will erase all of the data on your Kindle Paperwhite, including your books, settings, Wi-Fi networks, and personal information. This will restore your device to its original, out-of-the-box state. A factory reset is often used if your Kindle is still having problems after a soft reset, or if you are selling or giving away your device and want to erase your personal information.

Before performing a factory reset, ensure that you back up any important content, either by syncing it to your Amazon account or transferring it to a computer.

Steps for a Factory Reset:

1. **Open the Settings Menu**: From the Home screen, tap the menu icon (three horizontal lines) in the top-right corner and select "Settings."

2. **Go to Device Options**: Scroll down and tap "Device Options."

3. **Select Reset**: Tap on the "Reset" option, which is usually located at the bottom of the menu.

4. **Confirm the Reset**: You will be prompted to confirm that you want to erase all content and settings. Tap "Yes" to begin the reset process.

The reset process may take a few minutes to complete. After the reset, your Kindle Paperwhite will restart and guide you through the initial setup process as if it were a new device.

When to Use a Factory Reset

- **Persistent Software Issues**: If your Kindle is still malfunctioning after performing a soft reset, a factory reset might be necessary.
- **Selling or Giving Away Your Kindle**: If you're planning to sell or give away your Kindle, a factory reset will remove all personal information and ensure that the new owner can set it up as a new device.
- **Restoring to Default Settings**: If you've made too many changes to the device's settings or have trouble troubleshooting a particular problem, a factory reset will restore the device to its original settings.

Important Considerations Before Resetting

- **Back Up Your Data**: A factory reset erases all content from your Kindle, so it's crucial to back up your books, settings, and other data to your Amazon account or transfer them to another device.

- **Re-register Your Kindle**: After a factory reset, you'll need to sign in again with your Amazon account to restore your library and settings. Make sure you have your Amazon account details handy before resetting.
- **Software Updates**: After performing a reset, you might need to update your Kindle's software to the latest version. You can check for updates in the settings menu.

Contacting Amazon Support

If you're experiencing issues with your Kindle Paperwhite that cannot be resolved through troubleshooting or resets, or if you have questions about your device, Amazon Support is available to assist you. Amazon offers various support options to help you resolve problems quickly and efficiently. Here's how you can get in touch with Amazon Support:

1. Amazon Help & Customer Service

The first place to look for assistance is the **Amazon Help & Customer Service** page. Here you can find solutions to common issues, step-by-step troubleshooting guides, and links to contact Amazon support directly.

Steps to Access Amazon Help:

1. **Visit the Amazon Website**: Go to www.amazon.com (or your local Amazon site).

2. **Scroll to the Bottom**: On the homepage, scroll to the bottom and click on **"Customer Service"** under the "Let Us Help You" section.

3. **Search for Your Issue**: Use the search bar to look for solutions related to your Kindle Paperwhite. You can search for specific issues like "Kindle Paperwhite not charging" or "how to reset Kindle."

4. **Follow the Instructions**: If you find a solution, follow the provided steps to fix the problem.

If you can't find an answer to your issue, you can move on to the next step of contacting Amazon support directly.

2. Contacting Amazon Support via Chat or Email

Amazon provides options for contacting support via **chat** or **email,** allowing you to get personalized assistance.

Steps for Chat or Email Support:

1. **Go to the "Contact Us" Page**: In the Customer Service section, click on **"Contact Us"** to be directed to a page where you can choose the type of assistance you need.

2. **Select Kindle Support**: Choose "Devices and Digital Services," then select "Kindle" from the options.

3. **Choose a Contact Method**: You will be given a few options to reach Amazon support:

   Chat: Amazon's support chat system will connect you with an agent who can help you troubleshoot or resolve your issue.

   Email: If you prefer email communication, you can send your issue to Amazon Support, and they will respond within a specified time.

3. Contacting Amazon Support via Phone

If you prefer speaking with an Amazon support representative over the phone, you can request a call.

This option is especially useful if you need detailed assistance or need help with a complex issue.

Steps to Request a Phone Call:

1. **Go to the "Contact Us" Page**: As before, navigate to the "Contact Us" page in Amazon's Customer Service section.

2. **Choose "Phone":** After selecting "Kindle" and your issue, you will be given the option to choose **"Phone"** for a callback.

3. **Enter Your Phone Number**: You'll need to provide your phone number so that Amazon can call you. Choose the most convenient time for them to reach you.

4. **Wait for the Call**: Once you submit your phone number, an Amazon support representative will call you to assist with your Kindle issue.

4. **Kindle Support Pages**

Amazon also provides dedicated Kindle support pages, where you can find answers to many common Kindle-related questions, including device setup, troubleshooting, syncing, and more.

How to Access Kindle Support Pages:

1. **Visit the Kindle Support Site**: Go to the Kindle Support section of Amazon's website at https://www.amazon.com/gp/help/customer/display.html?nodeId=200127470.

2. **Browse Topics**: Browse through categories such as "Setting Up Your Kindle," "Device Features," "Troubleshooting," and "Account and Kindle Store" to find helpful articles.

3. **Check for Solutions**: You may find detailed guides and FAQs that can resolve your problem without the need to contact support directly.

5. **Amazon Forums and Communities**

Another option is to explore Amazon's **community forums** where users and experts discuss common Kindle Paperwhite issues and solutions. You can often find helpful tips from other Kindle owners who have experienced similar problems.

Accessing Amazon Forums:

1. **Go to the Amazon Community**: Visit [Amazon's Kindle Forum](https://www.amazon.com/forum/kindle).

2. **Search for Your Issue**: Use the search function to look for topics related to your problem or browse through existing threads to find advice and solutions.

3. **Post a Question**: If you don't find an answer, you can post a question to the community, and fellow users or Amazon moderators may respond.

6. Social Media Support

Amazon also offers support through their social media channels, including **Twitter**. You can tweet **@AmazonHelp**, where a representative will assist you with your Kindle-related issue.

Steps to Reach Out on Twitter:

1. **Open Twitter**: Open the Twitter app or visit the Twitter website.

2. **Tweet @AmazonHelp**: Send a message to **@AmazonHelp** with a description of your issue.

3. **Wait for a Response**: Amazon's support team will typically respond within a few hours to offer assistance.

7. Amazon's Return or Replacement Policy

If your Kindle Paperwhite is defective or has a hardware issue that cannot be fixed by support, Amazon offers a

return or replacement policy. You can initiate a return or exchange through your Amazon account.

Steps to Return or Replace Your Kindle Paperwhite:

1. **Go to Your Orders**: Log into your Amazon account and go to "Your Orders."

2. **Select the Kindle Paperwhite**: Find the Kindle Paperwhite in your order history.

3. **Request a Return or Replacement**: Choose the option to return or replace your device. Follow the instructions for returning the device and receiving a replacement or refund.

Frequently Asked Questions (FAQ)

1. How do I turn on my Kindle Paperwhite?

To turn on your Kindle Paperwhite, press and hold the power button for a few seconds until the screen lights up. The power button is typically located at the bottom or back of the device.

2. How do I charge my Kindle Paperwhite?

To charge your Kindle Paperwhite, use the included USB cable and plug it into a power source such as a wall charger or a USB port on your computer. The Kindle can take several hours to fully charge, depending on the power source.

3. Can I read books on my Kindle Paperwhite without Wi-Fi?

Yes, once you've downloaded books to your Kindle, you can read them offline. Wi-Fi is only needed to download new content, sync your library, or access online features such as Kindle Store browsing.

4. How do I connect my Kindle Paperwhite to Wi-Fi?

Go to the Home screen, tap the menu icon (three lines), and select "Settings." Under "Wi-Fi Networks," select your network and enter the password to connect. If you need help with Wi-Fi connection, check your router settings or reset your Kindle's network connections.

5. Can I read documents other than books on my Kindle Paperwhite?

Yes, you can upload documents such as PDFs, Word files, and other supported formats to your Kindle via USB or email them to your Kindle's unique email address. Once synced, these documents will appear in your library.

6. How do I change the font size or style on my Kindle Paperwhite?

To adjust the font size or style, open a book, tap the top of the screen to bring up the reading menu, then tap the "Aa" button. From there, you can customize the font style, size, line spacing, and margins according to your preference.

7. How can I highlight text or add notes?

To highlight text, press and hold on a word in the book, and drag the handles to select the text you want to highlight. Once selected, tap "Highlight." To add a note, after selecting the text, tap "Note" and type your note.

8. How do I sync my Kindle Paperwhite with my Amazon account?

To sync your Kindle with your Amazon account, ensure you're connected to Wi-Fi. From the Home screen, tap the menu icon, go to "Sync and Check for Items," and it will automatically sync your Kindle library and content with your Amazon account.

9. How do I update my Kindle Paperwhite's software?

To update your Kindle, go to the "Settings" menu, tap "Device Options," and select "Update Your Kindle" if an update is available. Make sure your Kindle is connected to Wi-Fi and has enough battery charge before starting the update.

10. How do I reset my Kindle Paperwhite?

If your Kindle is frozen or experiencing issues, you can perform a soft reset by holding the power button for about 40 seconds until the device restarts. For a more serious issue, you can perform a factory reset by going to "Settings" > "Device Options" > "Reset."

11. How do I transfer content from an old Kindle to my new Kindle Paperwhite?

To transfer content, ensure both devices are registered to the same Amazon account. From your old Kindle, sync your library to Amazon's cloud. On your new Kindle, connect to Wi-Fi and sync it to download the content from your cloud library.

12. Why is my Kindle Paperwhite not charging?

If your Kindle Paperwhite isn't charging, check the charging cable and adapter for any damage. Try using a different cable or charging source. Also, ensure the charging port is clean and free of debris. If the issue persists, consider performing a reset or contacting Amazon support.

13. How do I delete books from my Kindle Paperwhite?

To delete a book, go to your library, tap and hold the book cover, and select "Remove from Device." This will delete it from the Kindle but leave it in your cloud library so you can download it again if needed.

14. How do I set up Kindle Paperwhite for kids?

You can set up a Kindle Paperwhite for kids by creating a profile in **Amazon Kids**. This lets you customize the reading experience for children, including access to age-appropriate content and setting time limits for reading.

15. Can I use my Kindle Paperwhite in the dark?

Yes, the Kindle Paperwhite comes with built-in adjustable lighting that allows you to read in the dark without straining your eyes. You can adjust the brightness level according to your preference by tapping the top of the screen and using the brightness slider.

16. How do I manage my Kindle Paperwhite's storage?

To manage storage, go to "Settings" > "Device Options" > "Storage" to view the available space. You can delete old content or move it to the cloud to free up space. You can also manage downloaded books and documents via the "Manage Your Content and Devices" page on Amazon.

17. What should I do if my Kindle Paperwhite is frozen?

If your Kindle Paperwhite is frozen, perform a soft reset by holding the power button for 40 seconds until the screen goes black and the device restarts. This can resolve most freezing issues.

18. How can I contact Amazon customer support for my Kindle Paperwhite?

If you need further assistance, you can contact Amazon support via the Kindle help section in the Amazon app or website. You can also chat with a representative or request a call for more personalized support.

www.ingramcontent.com/pod-product-compliance
Lightning Source LLC
LaVergne TN
LVHW022347060326
832902LV00022B/4287